# Fair vs Equal

# Fair vs Equal

## Facing the Barriers to Technology Integration in Our Schools

Michele Wages

ROWMAN & LITTLEFIELD
Lanham • Boulder • New York • London

Published by Rowman & Littlefield
An imprint of The Rowman & Littlefield Publishing Group, Inc.
4501 Forbes Boulevard, Suite 200, Lanham, Maryland 20706
www.rowman.com

6 Tinworth Street, London SE11 5AL, United Kingdom

Copyright © 2021 by Michele Wages

*All rights reserved.* No part of this book may be reproduced in any form or by any electronic or mechanical means, including information storage and retrieval systems, without written permission from the publisher, except by a reviewer who may quote passages in a review.

British Library Cataloguing in Publication Information Available

Library of Congress Control Number: 2020948896

ISBN 9781475857382 (cloth) | ISBN 9781475857399 (pbk.) | ISBN 9781475857405 (epub)

# Contents

| | | |
|---|---|---|
| Foreword | | vii |
| Background | | ix |
| Introduction | | xi |
| 1 | Cost/Lack of Resources | 1 |
| 2 | Solution | 7 |
| 3 | Lack of Effective Knowledge and Training | 17 |
| 4 | Solution | 21 |
| 5 | Attitudes and Beliefs | 27 |
| 6 | Solutions | 31 |
| 7 | Lack of Computing Skills | 37 |
| 8 | Solutions | 43 |
| 9 | Infrastructure | 51 |
| 10 | Solution | 55 |
| 11 | High Stakes Assessment | 61 |
| 12 | Solution | 69 |
| Conclusion: So Where Do We Start? | | 75 |
| References | | 79 |
| About the Author | | 87 |

# Foreword

Is it a school's fault that a child is not prepared for the twenty-first century or is it the fault of a system that is neither fair nor equal? As a technology professional for the past thirteen years, I have witnessed tremendous advances in the digital field. Yet schools do not have the ability to keep up with the latest trends, and students are left ill-prepared for the future they will be thrown into.

Businesses claim that people entering the work force, even with a college degree do not have the skills needed to be successful in a technology career. Even with the increase in the digital native population and the dependence on computer networks, basic twenty-first-century skills are almost nonexistent in the graduating workforce.

This book provides a valuable insight to the most common challenges that schools face when trying to integrate twenty-first-century skills into their learning environment. Although many believe that finances are the primary reason, it is often the lack of knowledge and training that play the biggest role in fair and equitable technology integration. Low socio-economic districts also face challenges with crumbling building architecture as well as proper electrical systems that support technology.

Dr. Wages follows each chapter of barriers with possible solutions that can be easily implemented and support the development of a sound foundation for technology integration. It is important to keep in mind that effective integration of technology systems cannot happen immediately. The solutions provided in this book provide educational systems a place to start based on their current needs and to make advancements towards the ultimate goal of not only incorporating twenty-first-century skills into their learning environments but also leveling the playing field in technology integration.

Jonathan Parker<br>
Professional and Digital Learning Coordinator

# Background

**THE ROLE OF SOCIAL MEDIA AS A LEARNING TOOL**

Even though the benefits of integrating technology into our schools are numerous, the obstacles seem to outnumber the assets. If you ask students who their favorite teacher is, they will probably name the one who's constantly present on Facebook, answering their questions and posting links to content that makes learning fun. However, with the rise of social media in the classroom the focus is far more than how many people "like" your posts.

The collaborative environment and open forum that social media encourages, along with the rapid-pace of information sharing that it facilitates, means that students can accelerate the development of their creative, critical thinking, and communication processes in certain ways when they use it.

Social media promotes self-directed learning, which prepares students to search for answers and make decisions independently. When reinforced in a classroom setting, these social media skills can be guided and refined to produce better learning outcomes and increase critical awareness. Social media also allows students more freedom to connect and collaborate beyond the physical classroom, which means students anywhere can start to experience the globally connected world long before they enter the workforce.

Within social learning, students participate directly in their own learning rather than passively absorbing information they will most likely forget once the exam is over. Social media shapes and presents information in a way that makes sense and excites students more than traditional tools do, whether it is through a shared article with comment functionality, a livestream of an important event, a survey related to course materials, or a question posed to a broader community.

Furthermore, sharing posts and information with other students rather than simply submitting assignments to the teacher, promotes deeper engagement and better performance from all students. If students know from the start that they and their peers will interact with course materials and each other on various social media platforms, they may put in more effort to both their work and online presence.

But is there a downside to technology integration? Are digital devices dominating classrooms and distracting students from lessons? Are the new technologies causing the role of the educator to shift causing a real uncomfortableness as they are being forced to modify their approaches to teaching?

There are cons according to Himmelsbach (2019) in which I will also incorporate my own experience. I recently went out to eat with some friends. As I looked around the restaurant, I was astonished at the number of people attached to their cell phones. Few tables actually had people interacting in conversations with those sitting right across from them. "Is technology creating a generation of people that are disconnected from social interactions?" (Himmelsbach, 2019).

One would think that with all the educational apps available today reaching in the thousands; students' success is merely just a click away. Just plugging a child into a device however, is not a solution. Professional development, insightful implementation, and continual engagement must be combined with technology in order for integration to be successful.

It is easy for school leaders to demand that teachers and students must use the district's licensed apps continuously, but the reality is that most of the apps purchased are not correlated with the curriculum's learning outcomes. If districts continue to claim that they are data-driven then they must train teachers about intentional tracking and assessing data of usage rates and compare them to student success.

As simplistic as it may seem, districts should never just buy something, let it run and never analyze if the money spent truly makes an impact on student learning. Yet believe it or not, this is exactly what is happening in today's schools.

The increase in access to digital resources has increased the incidence of plagiarism and cheating by students in our schools. Teachers are frustrated at the ease at which students can access answers to questions or cut and paste information. For this reason, teachers have become digital policemen, taking up digital devices as students enter the classroom in order to prevent or at least decrease these incidences. However, home use is not as supervised and essay assignments have been riddled with resources not properly cited. Teachers are ill-prepared and schools underfunded to address the increasing technology availability in today's world.

# Introduction

As educators, the importance of teaching basic skills like reading, writing, and math has never been more at the forefront than today. What many policy makers don't seem to realize is that if we only provide these basics, then a huge gap in knowledge and skills develops that leave students short-changed on skills needed to function successfully in twenty-first-century workplace.

The rapid evolution and availability of technologies is just one of many issues. School boards make decisions about which technologies are permissible and available and provide an approved list that teachers must make a decision about which, if any, of them they will incorporate into their classroom. According to Hayden et al. (2011), it is unfortunate that "the technologies that are least used have the greatest impact on student engagement."

Today's educators are responsible for teaching their students skills in order to be effective citizens, workers, and leaders in society. In order to be successful, skills in critical thinking, communication, collaboration, and creativity must be incorporated into daily lessons.

Although technology helps with the management of tasks and provides an increased level of accuracy and speed, it also plays a major role because of its ability to bring real world environments into the classroom and streamline students' connections to a globally competitive workforce.

Even with most being enthusiastic about the role that technology can play in improving learning, many still feel unprepared to take advantage of digital tools in the classroom. The persistent barriers include too few computers and a lack of technical support, and inadequate professional development runs rampant in our schools.

Although education technology has been growing rapidly over recent years, you can barely imagine going hours without using some sort of technology. Yet, many of the classrooms across the United States find carts of brand new iPads and laptops, as well as computer labs being used infrequently or not at all.

According to Ron (2018), "In more than half of classrooms, there is no evidence students are using technology to gather, evaluate or use information for learning. In 2/3 of classrooms, there is no evidence students use it to solve problems, conduct research, or work collaboratively."

Even with the advantages of information being accessed immediately and its results in helping come up with solutions quickly, one has to wonder if we aren't creating lazy thinkers. By this I mean if they are not using their brains at full capacity including problem-solving calculations, writing techniques, and other things are completed by smart devices and applications are we creating students and eventually adults that are overly dependent on the assistance of smart machines? They become reliant on all the programs with their grammar, spelling, and punctuation error corrections, but when it comes time to actually put pen to paper, they are like deer caught in the headlights.

As you can see, the barriers to teachers implementing technology are many and they go much deeper than money factors. This book will dive further into six main barriers to technology integration in today's schools. Each barrier is followed by a chapter that explores possible solutions based on case studies and researched strategies.

*Chapter 1*

# Cost/Lack of Resources

> *Digital equity is a condition in which all individuals and communities have the information technology capacity needed for full participation in our society, democracy and economy*
>
> —National Digital Inclusive Alliance

It may come as a surprise to you that although technology in the classroom has grown at a rapid pace throughout the years, there are still some classrooms struggling to keep up with digital resources in our school systems.

Today's digital resources help students collaborate within, as well as beyond the school walls, and yet a surprising number of schools' classrooms are not fully integrated into technology. The greatest obstacle for the failure of educational technology (Ed-tech) integration is quite simply, the cost. How schools spend their money on technology varies widely across the United States and finds some more fortunate districts on the receiving end of grants and parental donations while others barely scrape by through tapping the local, state, and federal governments for funding. As the gap in technology gets larger in high poverty districts, catching up will require even more help from federal government as state aid and local property tax supplements decrease.

As Garland (2014) states, "The median school today pays $25 per megabit per month for their bandwidth, which is like you paying $500 a month for your Internet service." In addition, "A quarter of districts pay more than $100 per megabit a month" (Garland, 2014).

According to Nagel (2014), "Spending on high tech devices in schools reached $13 billion worldwide in 2013, with the U.S. spending more than

$4 billion that year on mobile devices alone. Overall education technology spending globally will reach $19 billion by 2019."

It is quite an investment to incorporate Ed-tech, and local government already has spent more than they had hoped in order to provide schools what little they already have, let alone keep up with the rising needs and maintenance costs including teacher training in effectively using technology in their classroom. Many schools find themselves so bound by their budget that they have allowed personal devices to be brought into the classroom by students, but this creates additional problems in the fact that all students do not have compatible devices such as the variety of iPads, tablets, and Smartboards in their classroom.

Ed-tech also faces another problem which has been labeled "technological poverty." This is evident in low-income school districts in which students and campuses do not have access to today's technology in terms of devices, internet access, or computer literacy skills. To complicate this even further, if Ed-tech is available in these schools, the majority of students either do not have compatible devices or internet service in their home. This results in homework not being able to be completed, and teachers becoming more and more frustrated.

According to International Society for Technology in Education as cited by Herold (2016) in their analysis entitled Teachers and Technology Use in the Classroom: Exclusive survey results, "Teachers who are most confident about educational technology tend to work in low poverty and suburban schools, bringing those students a wide range of experiences and potential benefits that other young people may lack." These confident teachers have students that spend twice as much class time using digital resources than students with less confident teachers. It was also concluded in this survey that teachers' confidence in Ed-tech aligns with district sets of behaviors, perceptions, and choices for the classroom. Add this to the unfortunate existence of technological poverty and we see an even larger gap in the digital divide in K-12 across the United States.

Whether we are looking at access to high-speed internet or ways technology devices are being used, the reality is that urban and poor students are at a huge disadvantage. According to Zhao (2017) a 2010 National Center for Education Statistics report found nearly every U.S. school having a least one instructional computer with internet access, with a ratio of 3:1students for every computer connected to the internet. Unfortunately for schools in high-poverty areas, these numbers are much lower. One such example is Bronzeville Scholastic Institute in which their nearly one thousand ninth graders share twenty-four computers.

This digital divide (the definition used for the purpose of this book, refers to whether classrooms had computers connected to the internet) may cause you to ask yourself how a slight difference in the use of active technology and personalized learning approaches could really cause such a deficit in learning for a student. Some examples of how this happens from Zhao (2017) is in the comparison in which only 5 percent of less confident teachers that utilize some sort of website creation or editing tools in their classroom compares to 16 percent of more confident teachers.

Another example is only 10 percent of less confident teachers access online videos to enhance instruction, while 25 percent of the confident teacher utilize videos as part of their instructional make-up. The use of web-based collaboration tools happens approximately 13 percent of class time in a less confident teacher versus 23 percent in their more confident counterpart. These differences are only based on one school year. Students spend twelve years in their school journey, and for those in less privileged schools this is just the beginning of the huge technology gap.

It is true that technology is becoming more affordable and internet access seems increasingly present, but the reality is that according to Ziekuhr and Smith (2012), as reported by the Pew Internet and American Life Project, the more prevalent are still more likely than others to have dependable access to high-speed digital resources.

Believe it or not, a digital divide is not just about access to hardware and high-speed internet and has tremendous consequences when it comes to education. Especially for students in low-income school districts, this lack of access to technology hinders them from not only learning tech-skills but also puts them at a huge disadvantage in the job market as they become adults.

According to the 2012 Pew report entitled Digital Differences, "only 62% of people in households making less than $30,000 a year used the internet, while in those making $50,000-74,999 that percentage jumped to 90." The gap in the access to high-speed internet also exists. According to this same Pew report, "only 49% of African Americans and 51% of Hispanics have high-speed internet at home, as compared with 66% of Caucasians." Since speed of the internet has a direct effect on the ability to stream video and access media, this is a significant difference.

If that wasn't convincing enough, according to McKay (2018), in 2014, 3.9 million people were working in the IT industry with a growth of another 12 percent (488,500 jobs) predicted between 2014 and 2024. The median average salary of an IT professional is $82,860. If your child was not prepared to enter a technology-dominated workforce, would your perception of the technology divide be more urgent? Does the cost of technology integration in our schools seem a bit more necessary?

According to a report by Smith et al. (2011) based on research from the Pew Internet & American Life Project, "most of the mobile devices owned by students are probably cell phones, whose educational utility is limited. Even More relevant, Pew also found that "only 70 percent of students at community colleges had a laptop or desktop computer and only 78% had broadband at home and could connect wirelessly."

**Teachers and administrators do not view computer science education as a high priority.**
Computer science is not included in the top 5 of the priority requirements list in education. In fact, Smith (2011) stated that in spite of 7 percent of principals and 6 percent of superintendents reporting that the demand for it was high, less than one-third of those same administrators agreed that computer science education was not a priority in their district.

If that wasn't bad enough, according to Herold (2017), students in high poverty schools are less likely than their counterparts in wealthier schools to have teachers receiving training in how to integrate technology into their classroom.

**Budgets and competing interests edge out computer science learning opportunities**
The primary reason for not offering computer science classes is due to the limited time to devote to these classes and the reality that they are not tied to standardized testing requirements. Another reason often heard is that the budget is limited for these courses and the equipment and software that would be needed.

In addition, even if computer science classes are offered, the fact is that technology is expensive. For poorer school districts, the only way digital devices can be afforded is if they are donated. Although greatly appreciated, most of these devices have been refurbished and over five years old. This makes them ideal for teaching fundamental skills but not effective in the use of the latest technologies. Missing out on the advanced skills and newest technologies leaves students entering college or the working world left at a disadvantage.

**Existing computer science offerings lack core elements.**
Then there are those districts according to Lynch (2018) that do offer computer science courses in which approximately 47 percent of the surveyed principals confess that computer programming and coding—core elements of computer science—are not part of the coursework.

Educators are aware that schools and districts, for the most part, have limited money to spend on technology. This brings about the need to find ways to cut corners and often results more times than not, in buying software and devices because they are a good deal. These good deals frequently do not translate into useful learning and do not integrate with current systems that are already in place in a district. This causes implementation and new systems to lie dormant and unused.

The upgrading and implementation of technology never stops. Just as people's needs change almost every day, so does digital integration. School budgets do not accommodate for all expenses in the purchasing of new prototypes, and hence are forced to use outdated technology.

In the case of poorer school districts this creates a climate of unequal opportunities when compared to their wealthier counterparts. It is no wonder that administrators are left searching for ways to cut corners, but the problem lies in how it sacrifices the integrity of education for students.

So the question arises as to why educational systems misspend money on educational technology. According to Lynch (2018), "K-12 schools don't always appreciate what type of technology they really need." Few, if any, attend conferences that help keep them informed about the latest and greatest in technology. Many get swayed by representatives' smooth-talking and promises or by a brand name they are familiar with when they have no clue about the products themselves. Many of these items are not the right fit for K-12 schools, too expensive for the district in the long term and ineffective for students.

One of the most common misconceptions is that just having technology in the classroom will lead to it being used. The reality is that it is not in the availability of technology that is the problem, "the real issue is that K-12 schools are spending far too much money on products that may not be the best choice based on the school's current curriculum and student population" (Lynch, 2018).

*Chapter 2*

# Solution

*Digital equity is the civil rights issue of our time.*

—Keith Krueger

One of the goals of educators should be to assist in bridging the digital divide in order for all students to acquire the technological skills they need to become college and career ready.

Yet teachers are not given a say in most technology purchases. Who knows better what is feasible and will work in the classroom than the teacher? Allowing teachers and students if possible, to be included in the decision making of technology purchases instead of these decisions being left up to those farthest away from the classroom at the district office, would be a great start to better utilization of technology (Lynch, 2018).

The majority of today's students are considered digital natives, having grown up totally immersed in technology. Others however, for various reasons, have not been able to reach their technological skills level. So what do these less privileged students do?

**Innovate with the tools you already have.**

One such teacher in Oklahoma found herself in a classroom where she had only one desktop for her students, a class set of graphing calculators, a projector, her school issued laptop, and a mobile cart of laptops which she shared with three other teachers. Microsoft Office and web browsers were available on the PCs. Instead of throwing up her hands in defeat, she started with what she had and assigned real-world problems to put the digital tools to work.

Analyzing local cell phone plans, the students used algebra formulas to determine which plan was the best value. Role-playing as consultants, electronic presentations were created by the students including graphs in order to explain their findings to their families.

**Seek out free-easy to use digital resources.**

As one kinder teacher proved, you don't need a lot to incorporate technology. Utilizing a free app known as VoiceThread, a tool for creating collaborative multimedia slide shows, she provided an opportunity for students in Australia to comment on her students' work in New Hampshire.

According to Nekilan (2018), the nine best free apps for teachers in 2018 include:

- **Class Dojo:** Great for communication for teachers, students, and parents. You can send and share videos, photos, and announcements.
- **Teacher's Assistant Pro:** Keep track of student's actions, behaviors, and achievements in the classroom.
- **Educreations:** A whiteboard and a screencasting tool. Teachers can create and show short instructional videos and share the videos with students quickly and easily.
- **Blackboard:** Students stay updated with content, assignments, tests, grades, and participation. Teachers can video chat with students, which is perfect for tutoring.
- **State the States**: Teach students all fifty states, location to capitals.
- **Virtual Nerd Mobile Math**: Guides both teacher and student interactive tutorials, lesson videos for middle and high school.
- **SeeSaw:** Student-driven portfolio. Shows how to create, collaborate, reflect, and share as well as invites families to view and understand the student's learning.
- **Kahoot:** Included fun learning games, quizzes for teachers to set up for their students which can also be used for homework and tutoring.
- **Classtree for Parent-Teacher Communication:** Instead of filling out paper form for conferences, this is an easy way to show where the child is at school in terms of behavior and learning. It also includes features for e-signatures, consents, and real-time reporting.

1. **Overcome your fear of the unknown.**

Teachers fear of learning something new is still the main hurdle to technology integration. Through collaborative Professional Learning Communities (PLCs), conducted during the school day, schools across the United States provided time for teachers to discuss issues that relate to student learning including technology integration. This also provided a venue for educators to see other educators teaching in different ways in order for new practices to take hold.

## 2. Start with small, fast projects that enhance learning.

Safe learning activities that help connect new content with what the students are already doing should be incorporated. For example: Google Lit trips combine place-based literature study with the satellite technology of Google Earth. The program has a preloaded list of books that appear on the majority of district's reading lists such as The Grapes of Wrath. Once you click on the place marks, there are choices of various video clips and other images that make the story more real for students.

## 3. Start with something familiar and close to what students are already doing but so different that it can be portal to new possibilities.

For example: WebQuests has an abundance of inquiry-oriented lessons that teachers can preselect while also including higher-order questions about specific topics. This also provides an opportunity for teachers to learn side by side with students in the classroom as they explore technology. One suggestion here is in order for barriers of limited technology access, insufficient time, or adequate technical support to be broken down, it is important for others to see the evidence that technology is being used successfully.

## MAXIMIZING USE OF FREE TECHNOLOGY RESOURCES

Even with the presence of the growing digital divide, subscription of home broadband occurs in only 71 percent of American households (Goodman, 2013).

In Montgomery County, Virginia, a superintendent used Moodle to launch online learning systems which allow students to use curriculum materials online. Today, schools have multiple leaning management systems to choose from that enable the sharing of information and provide access to curriculum online.

Utilizing Google Drive, teachers can create and save lessons as well as share them with staff across and outside of the district. This provides convenient, immediate opportunities for vertical and horizontal planning within a campus or across the district while also providing new teachers models of good lesson planning, instructional strategies, supplemental resources, and time management skills. These lessons can remain online for an entire year, which allows administrators and instructional coaches to access them for evaluations, monitoring and observing and to track instructional improvements of teachers.

Many schools are attempting to implement a 1:1 program, supplying an internet-connected device such as a laptop, tablet, or similar device for each student. The focus here is to provide instructional strategies in multiple formats that support differentiated instruction, project-based learning, flipped classrooms, and enhance collaboration and communication. What is interesting is that according to Richardson, McLeod, and Sauers (2013), nearly every study of 1:1 programs revealed that "unless the students take devices home, there is little demonstrable impact on learning."

The belief behind this is that as popular as this implementation is, students can only continue learning outside of school based upon home internet connectivity.

Although learning management systems such as Moodle, Schoology, Google Applications, and Office 365 replace and improve upon traditional print textbooks, they do require internal connectivity and are designed to be used while online as do web-based e-books such as Tumblebooks, Razkids, and the International Children's digital library.

In addition, research and exploration on most school topics require real-time search engines such as Google, Google Scholar, or video demonstrations and presentations that can be found on YouTube. Even though a device can be loaded with programs such as Google Docs, videos, and articles, this information takes up much of the device's memory as do games and other learning applications which can cause issues such as programs having to be deleted and downloaded constantly as the curriculum and instructional focus changes throughout the year.

It costs about $100 a year per student for a school to provide a device such as a Chromebook or iPad which does not include the cost of internet connectivity and network licenses which when combined is an amount most school budgets cannot afford.

**So how can schools provide internet access to students whose families do not have the resources to complete the assignments sent home.**

Obviously, reducing the need for home internet connectivity would be one of the easiest ways to close the digital divide. Internet drives and flash-based memory storage such as with laptops, iPads and other tablets can be chosen for school devices. But his can also add another barrier in that instructional materials and supplemental resources must be able to be downloaded according to copyright laws and devices need to have enough memory for storage of these materials. In schools where computers are shared between content areas and grade levels, this could cause even more of a budget issue requiring more memory or more devices as well as internal conflict between staff as to whose programs are more important to download.

For example: To aid in diminishing the "homework gap," The School City of Mishawaka teamed up with Sprint in handing out free smartphones to high school students with little or no internet access at home. This increased communication between students and teachers resulting in more homework being completed.

On the bright side, there are tools like Microsoft 365 and Google applications that have both online and offline versions of programs that students and teachers can use.

Teachers can also examine whether their students' homework actually requires internet access. For example, e-books and videos that have been downloaded onto their devices do not need internet access, so the teacher needs to determine if access to the internet is truly needed for the learning that is desired.

But there is one unfortunate downside as Piedmont City School District discovered in which limiting the amount of internet access, although financially doable, did not meet the district's goal of the technology 1:1 device program that the superintendent and board voted into place for the school year (Schwartz, 2014).

## EXPAND ACCESS AT SCHOOL

Being proactive in expanding school-wide internet access is a high priority for most schools. By providing access during the school day, where students work both before and after school including places such as study hall, the cafeteria and the library as well as during the school day may be an option to relieve some of this dilemma.

In large rural populated school districts, wireless connection has been added to school buses in order to provide "rolling study halls" for students during their commute to and from school as well as activities such as concerts and sporting events. Many internet providers offer a variety of "hot spot" portable 3/4G wireless access points, and students can check them out for home use (Cavanagh, 2014). One such example of this is the Coachella Valley Unified School District in California, where buses are wired so that students can complete their homework on their way to and from home (Bentley, 2018).

"Hotspot" buses have also been parked in mobile home parks and designated under-resourced neighborhoods at the end of the day in some school districts. This provides free internet access for these families during the evenings.

Another approach is to identify apartment complexes that house the highest concentrations of low-income students and provide wireless connections in their common areas for student use. Beware however as Childhood Internet

Protection Act (CIPA) filtering guidelines would apply to these connections which may limit their access.

According to Schrume (2018), some school districts "provide mobile devices for students to take home to level the access and provide for the connections, and others negotiate with local internet providers to lower the cost for families with students in the district."

One such example is Beekmantown Central School District in West Chazy, New York which has a hotspot program where students that are enrolled in any of its four schools are offered free wireless hotspot devices to those that do not have internet access at home. The district picks up the tab for both the device and the monthly access cost through an Extended Learning Time (ELT) grant.

## WORK WITH THE COMMUNITY

Yet another option is that places like public libraries, YMCA's, and many community centers where students spend a good amount of time offer free internet access. Also, don't forget about businesses like coffee shops, nail salons and retailers who also provide access to their customers to link into their wireless networks. The key here is informing students and parents about these options.

"Smart Partnerships" can be formed with local, state, national and international organizations (NGO's) as another strategy. Florence County School District 3 (Lake City, South Carolina) was the recipient of a $9.1 million grant over a five-year period from the U.S. Department of Education. The district used the funds to develop their C3 (Colleges, cultures and careers) project in order to offer new opportunities for students in which to develop career paths through integrating new skills and knowledge (Schrum, 2018).

## INFORM PARENTS ABOUT LOW-COST ACCESS

Nonprofit organizations that are affiliated with telecommunication providers are another avenue in providing affordable internet connectivity to low-income families. For a list of participating partnerships, one can log in to Everyoneon at https://www.everyoneon.org which is a national nonprofit organization that provides K-12 students with affordable internet access through partnerships with leading cable companies throughout the United States.

Although this option does not completely bridge the digital divide, it does narrow it by providing home connectivity for those in need, extending learning opportunities for children.

## REPRIORITIZE EXISTING FUNDS

According to O'Donnell (2017), in 2010, an urban school district in Connecticut where more than 70 percent of the students qualified for free and reduced price lunches wanted to put a single device program in place. Meriden Public Schools realized that in order to compete in today's world, their students needed exposure to technology and so it was a priority. Over 8,000 students of their school received a device which in turn opened up endless opportunities such as online courses, adaptive software, and a peer-to-peer tech buddies program.

The director of Curriculum and Instructional Technology, Barbara Haeffner stated, "Once the district invested in the 1:1 device program, they began to save money on textbooks, paper and xeroxing and printing costs." Now, when they look to buy textbooks, the first question they ask publishers is whether it includes a digital component.

During the eight years of their technology commitment, Meriden Public Schools has been named a district of distinction and one of its elementary schools was named a model school.

## APPLY FOR GRANTS

Let's face it, technology costs money. That fact is not vanishing any time soon. One way schools can receive money is through grant opportunities. There are funds designated for using technology in the classroom and developing new learning technologies in public schools. Many districts are hopeful that bond referendums will fill the financial gap for implementing state of the art technology; however, bonds are voted on and paid by taxpayers and cannot be considered a sure thing in today's economy.

So how did Meriden Public Schools' digital transformation take place? As with most districts on a limited budget, administrators carefully trimmed their budget and began searching for outside funding sources. After careful research based on the districts' specific goals and objectives, they applied and received grant money from the Nellie May Education Foundation and Rise Education Foundation.

It is a tedious task to apply for grants. Not only is it time consuming and many times on going, but well worth the effort. Many districts hire a full- or part-time grant writer to offset the demands of the writing process. There are a variety of easy-to-use grant databases in which specific types of grants that meet specific district technology focuses. They include:

- Grants.gov includes a grants learning center that not only provides a list of available grants but also has tutorials on how to write a grant and sends out updates when new grant opportunities become available.

- Grant Watch informs readers as to what government and foundation grants are currently available through our user-friendly grants search and grant summaries.
- GrantSelect online database of funding opportunities such as grants (for programs, projects, planning, start-up, endowments, technical assistance, facilities, and equipment, etc.), awards, and fellowships, for example.
- GrantsAlert.com one stop shop to find current funding opportunities for your school, district, and community.
- Teach.com at https://teach.com/what/teachers-change-lives/grants-for-teachers a wide variety of sources available for funding educational initiatives. Grants, fellowships and scholarships are available for teachers who want to help their students.

## PROCURE GOVERNMENT FUNDING

Although you may be aware that in 2015, the U.S. Department of Education finalized state accountability plans for implementing The Every Student Succeeds Act (ESSA) and it was signed by President Obama. What you might not realize however, is that among other things, this law authorizes new funding streams that can help states and districts with this their investment in technology.

- Such allowances include the Student Support and Academic Enrichment block grant program. Through Title IV this allows up to 60 percent of funding to be used for innovative technology strategies.
- Title II funding focuses on technology for the use of data and for professional development.
- Title I flexibility, which provides broader initiatives to focus on in order to motivate state and district technology goals.

The Center for Digital Education (CDE) published a forty-page handbook providing guidance to states and districts. It is titled "ESSA, EdTech and the Future of Education," and provides insight on new opportunities that are available and suggestions on how to best integrate them into a district's vision of guiding teaching and learning.

## FUNDRAISE

Today's technology has broadened the access to a variety of audiences in which to raise funds. From Facebook to Twitter educators can transform a classroom in just a few clicks. Some easy, cost-effective and engaging fundraisers include:

- Crowdfunding: Donors Choose and Digital Wish are programs that can connect teachers with prospective donors and almost eliminates the tedious search process. Basically the process requires the educator to create a profile and then a wish list of technology items needed for a specific classroom or school project.
- Recycling fundraisers

Donors can choose which project they will support. The Crowdfunding page can also be shared through social media or include personal networks. A free program called FundingFactory, is another way classrooms can raise money by collecting empty toner and ink cartridges. Points are earned as the items are recycled and can be exchanged for educational technology or cash. One last source is "Awesome Fundraising Ideas: Recycling Fundraisers for School Trips" by Scholastica Travel Inc. which provides a list of additional recycling fundraisers that may better fit your needs.

## APPLY FOR TEACHER AWARDS

There are also a large bank of teacher award programs like the NEA Foundation's Awards for Teaching Excellence. This program provides cash prizes for winners to spend in their classroom.

Visit The New Teacher Project's (TNTP) list of 10 Awards for Great Teachers for more options.

## SECURE CORPORATE PARTNERSHIPS

To strengthen public-private partnerships, while also spurring innovation in education and learning through technology and research, there is Digital Promise, a nonprofit authorized by the U.S. Congress in which the belief is that multiple stakeholders need to work as partners in order to tackle technological challenges.

## LOOKING AHEAD

Although these charitable grants, fundraising campaigns, and corporate partnerships offer band-aid solutions to the digital divide the strength in them relies on the school's leadership. Teachers also play a vital role for without their support and motivation gains in technology cannot be made.

As for looking ahead, colleges need to take computer skills to the next level, one beyond the fundamentals. Digital document archiving, web page design, using a firewall, and setting up wireless networks are just a few of the skills needed to compete in today's job market. No longer can we rely on tech support located halfway around the world and are difficult to communicate with. Our students need these skills, and as educators, we need to provide them.

No single approach will address the multitude of facets making up today's digital inequity. Aiding in the successful narrowing of the digital gap is the knowledge our student's need and must include out of school context along with collaboration between educators, students, parents, and the entire community (Schrum, 2018).

*Chapter 3*

# Lack of Effective Knowledge and Training

> *The introduction of computers into schools was supposed to improve academic achievement and alter how teachers taught. Neither has occurred.*
>
> —Larry Cuban, Stanford University education professor

The truth of the matter is that if educational organizations do not have the budget to purchase digital devices, then they absolutely won't have the money to pay for training needed for teachers to use the devices. Successful integration of technology can only happen if teachers are properly trained, especially since many have not been exposed to or grown up using them like their students.

For most teachers who have been exposed to technology, few know how to use it properly in their classroom. Understanding appropriate pedagogy for practicing technology can be more important to effective instruction than technical mastery of technology. In other words, trainings need to incorporate less on what to do with the device and more on what to do through the device.

To address this, educational institutions have integrated courses and professional development trainings on the effective use of educational technology in the classroom. This has assisted educators as a whole, but particularly those that did not grow up with computers or the internet and are resistant to incorporating them for fear of failure or showing students their incompetence.

This can create a huge barrier in technology integration in three main ways:

**Lack of knowledge of specific technology**: We as humans find change sometimes to be overwhelming or frightening, and the same can be said for teachers and today's technology. The sad part is though that the more frightened or overwhelmed they are, and the less training available to them, the less likely they are to incorporate technology into their daily instruction.

For example, a teacher who does not have the basic skills such as saving information on to a home drive may not utilize any technology activities with their students. What usually happens is that specific technology is mandated by schools without verifying that teachers have the tools and skills to integrate it. Unfortunately, the end result is high dollar technology investment become underutilized or worst-case scenario, not used at all and teachers return to the old way of doing things.

In addition, those teachers at the secondary level may worry that their students are more adept to technology then they are and therefore are more reluctant to use it for fear of showing their lack of technological knowledge. This is why technology training is so important for teachers. Showing them not only how to use it but to use it effectively within the content curriculum is the key to integration.

**Inadequate knowledge of technology-supported pedagogy**: Then there are those teachers that understand how to use digital tools, but struggle with utilizing it effectively to improve instruction. The majority of professional development in technology is the instruction of the mechanics or basics of various applications and resources. Rarely does it address how to use it in supporting the curriculum. Technology is not designed to be used like a textbook in which teachers present from a PowerPoint presentation or just a drill and kill software.

In short, teachers are taught what it is, but not how to integrate it into the classroom. In the twenty-first century, technology integration is a transformation and thus, teachers need to know how technology can function within educational pedagogy and properly integrate it into the curriculum. Without the connection to pedagogy, technology integration serves no meaningful purpose. Transformation to 1 to 1 device integration does not happen just by giving each student a device. Teachers must utilize it with the goal of reaching higher-order teaching and learning.

**Insufficient knowledge of technology-related-classroom management**: "Classroom management has been identified as the most important factor influencing student learning" (Wang et al., 1993).

Many educators are unaware that the traditional classroom rules and procedures can also apply in a technology-integrated environment, but adaptations have to be made to accommodate for the digital tools (Lim et al., 2003).

One such example is in the case where a media specialist discusses rules such as the number of pages one can print out at a time, or the limits of time for each student to be logged in to a device. Without rules and limits, educators may find technology too cumbersome to manage and simply avoid its use.

Without additional time, teachers cannot find opportunities to add technology into their daily lesson plans and defer to their existing lesson plans. Teachers are very busy, and many will take the path of least resistance if not given the opportunity and time to learn how to best integrate the new materials and items into their lessons.

In education, there are those programs that require substantial classroom time in order to be fully utilized. In a world of high stakes testing, most educators are not willing to give up large chunks of instructional time. Even with this knowledge few teachers consistently receive updated explanations about how to exploit this or that application. This assists in the end result of creating useless technology.

In the case of a computer lab or library media center setting where there are a greater number of resources such as printers, scanners, recording devices and alike, the inadequate knowledge and lack of management rules can serve as a tremendous barrier.

It is imperative that media specialists be trained in both how to use these technologies and how to incorporate them into the curriculum along with the teachers. In many cases, the library media center is the primary place teachers go to access and check out various technology tools and if a librarian is not up to date on digital tools, it may lead to a lack of purchasing additional resources and assist in building the wall that prevents technology integration of the entire school.

Information is far from scarce in today's world, and the teacher's role is broadening every day. This can cause educators to be overwhelmed by the wealth of sources needed to create new knowledge for students.

Our society can no longer afford to think of education as being defined by four classroom walls but one of engagement, nimbleness, creativity, and commitment to action.

Differing perspectives can no longer be ignored, fixed, or eliminated in our global society; they have become norms of everyday work. Learning new things relies on our human survival abilities and putting together information to solve problems in abundantly different situations. This reflects in the demand of today's teachers to teach our children how to do this. Young people's success in our global community relies on their ability to develop the understandings, skills, and attributes to compete in a knowledge era.

It goes without saying that further research and progress needs to be made in the vital importance of computational literacy as well as cultural perspectives so that educators can better serve children across all disciplines of study, as well as their future citizenship responsibilities.

It is human nature to fall back into old certainties and return to what is familiar in the area of teaching and learning. The comfort of familiar routines provides us with a sense of control and order. The world, however, continues to evolve and in the case of technology, it happens exceedingly fast. Each day is unlike any other we have known before.

As with most fast-paced changes, many educators find themselves lacking confidence in their ability to think broadly with technology. According to Walker (2018), the average teacher in the United States in 2016 had fourteen years of experience and worked roughly fifty-three hours a week.

This results in many classroom teachers having less experience with computers in their own lives than their students who have grown up embedded in technology. In addition, few professional development trainings help teachers with the actual integration of technology into their teaching, leaving them feeling torn between knowing they should incorporate technology and not knowing how to do it.

Adding to the disconnect is the fact that according to the U.S. Department of Education (2016) the majority of academic and school leadership personnel have an average age of forty-eight years old and have even less experience with technology than their teachers and therefore cannot provide informed support in the infusion of technology in their buildings.

Yet another layer to this is the fact that most IT specialists are not educators. District-wide network designs and access are often determined by the year's budget along with what is standard, and easy to maintain and monitor instead of what is best for the students.

The reality of today is that although thousands of digital media objects and teacher-created lessons that claim meaningful technology integration exist, there truly are very few effective and authentic methods for infusing technology in an imaginative way into lessons for educators.

A final issue that relates to one discussed above is that good teachers are leaving the profession at a disturbing rate. Although pay is one reason, according to Adams (2017), about 90 percent of teacher vacancies nationwide are created by teachers leaving the profession for reasons other than retirement. One of the stated reasons is that they feel they were ill prepared for the job, especially in the case of those that took the nonstandard route to a credential. Alternative paths generally have considerably less coursework and fewer student teaching hour requirements than a university or credentialing program.

This combined with the lack of support and professional development leaves teachers who may even have technology expertise frustrated with the barriers they have to overcome in implementing what they feel is good for student learning.

## Chapter 4

# Solution

*The best training program in the world is absolutely worthless without the will to execute it properly, consistently, and with intensity.*

—John Romaniello

According to the New Media Consortium Horizon Report (2017), there are five key trends that will impact education over the next five years. Those included:

1. An increasing shift toward blended learning, online learning, and technology-driven collaborative learning;
2. The growth in the potential of social networks to allow teachers to engage students online;
3. Openness of educational resources and technology is "becoming a value";
4. Bring Your Own Device (BYOD) is becoming more common as the cost of technology drops for students; and
5. The role of the educator is being challenged as resources become more accessible on the Internet.

In order to motivate teachers, they have to see a clear connection between the content they are teaching and the technology to be used. Only within realizing its relevance will teachers incorporate technology into their day-to-day instruction.

Teachers fear unpredictability and have the perception that technology can increase this dramatically. The best place to start is by establishing clear rules regarding technology use from day one in the classroom.

There are several varieties of active learning. For example, experienced colleagues can serve as role models and mentors in having more novice teachers observe them during their implementation of technology. This allows the less experienced teacher to see the effective use of technology in daily instruction.

The timing of professional development is of vital importance with respect to the curriculum framework and teacher's lesson plans. Most districts provide technology training at the beginning of the school year when in reality it may be most effective to show it to them just a few weeks before it is needed based on the curriculum timeline. This will help teachers to become more likely to look at upcoming curriculum in order to integrate technology and it known as situational coaching.

Today's teachers need a variety of instructional methods as most will teach children growing up in a different age. Preservice teachers experience infusion of technology through college courses they take and also in observation and student teaching practicum in schools. The gap appears in the fact that the average educator in schools and university classrooms were not taught in a formal setting about digital learning, but had to explore it along the way while creating relevant learning opportunities for students, that they themselves never experienced.

In an article by Jacobson, Clifford and Friesen (2002), the faculty of education at the University of Calgary discusses their journey of innovation and revolution. The faculty did some research and found that as a general rule, "Teacher education programs were organized around an applied science model within which individual courses were framed by philosophical and theoretical content, and these in turn were followed by short-term practice teaching in schools."

In response to this research, the University of Calgary implemented a course of action focused on discontinuing its present teacher education programs that followed the model research exposed. Their plan was to replace it with a cohesive professional degree program model based on pedagogical knowledge while also incorporating cooperative problem-solving. This model valued not only the learner as a professional in the making but also provided a link that brought theory and practice closer together.

The updated, two-year Master of Teaching (MT) program at Calvary incorporated case study, field seminars, independent studies, and extensive field experiences replacing the outdated, discreet, lecture-based courses of the past. Within this modern model, equal amounts of time are divided for students between the campus and the field providing more relative links between the two.

While on the campus, students analyze case studies, take positions, and defend their perspective which encompasses an incentive for collaborative learning. The other half includes a field portion that engages students in a variety of educational settings where they face pragmatic issues that teachers and students encounter in today's classrooms.

Professional seminars are also incorporated in order to provide students the opportunity to reflect critically on themselves as future teachers and pursue information on topics and skills of particular interest.

By the fifth year of the newly updated program, Calvary's MT students "clearly demonstrated its capability to prepare teachers who are energetic, reflective, cooperative practitioners capable of solving problems, confronting new challenges, and taking and defending positions on complex issues" (Jacobson et al., 2002).

This restructuring supports the fact that preservice teachers need to experience learning environments that are digitally rich and inquiry-based not only in their coursework but also in their field placements. Changing the focus to teaching and thinking with technology moves the students beyond skill acquisition and incorporates relevant software application to create learning opportunities based on the real world of education.

The key in successful restructuring is to not approach it from a "fix teaching" mindset. Remember there are a tremendous number of talented veteran teachers out there that are used to producing excellent standardized testing scores and have consistently demonstrated their effective teaching in preparing students. Approaching these teachers with a radically changing mindset and pedagogy can leave a huge distaste in their mouths.

A way around the deflective approach is to visit classrooms of veteran teachers. Note what they do that makes them successful and build from that. Casually suggest a technology app that would make their good teaching even more efficient and effective. For example, Dropbox would facilitate the distribution of handouts for a teacher and Google Then as teachers become more comfortable and realize that technology can make things easier, they will be more likely to have future conversations about other digital tools.

Teachers also need to know that support is available and feel secure in knowing they will be accommodated when they reach out. The best way to do this is to meet them where they are. If they want to use Safari, for example, but another app has been developed that is far superior, remember the importance of the teacher's comfort level and start where they are.

Peers are often trusted by fellow teachers and can take the role of model and trainer. They are viewed as experienced and aware of daily issues faced in today's classrooms and thus less of a threat to a teacher's security.

All teachers work longer than the 7–3 schedule. According to Walker (2018), the average teacher in 2016 worked roughly fifty-three plus hours a week. As far as summers off, well I know few if any teachers that are not busy with some school-related activity during these months. With these facts in mind, it is highly suggested that May and June are the best months for effective training of technology concepts.

In the case of rolling out new digital devices such as ipads or laptops, Carey (2013), suggests handing them out at the end of the year giving educators the summer to play with and get comfortable with the tool. The home environment takes away the intimidation of someone standing over your shoulder and allows educators to work at their own pace in preparation for the fall.

Trusting teachers as the professionals they are is also important. Encourage teachers to make the device their own through downloading music, having administrative privileges, and merging their personal email on to the device. This promotes an extra level of comfort that comes with ownership. Of course, it goes without saying that parameters still need to be followed so that no illegal activities or questionable images and others are downloaded.

According to Carey (2013), providing the faculty the ability to intimately connect with their technology educators are provided the capacity to thoroughly explore and understand how the device works.

Programs with a low learning level are less intimidating and have minimal chances of crashing. The easier to use and understand, the better the chance teachers will use it and be curious about other applications versus becoming frustrated and quickly discard it

The most important thing to remember is to avoid a judgment role. Hesitant educators are often labeled as being lazy, stubborn, or simply lack creativity when it comes to adopting new technology. The truth is however, that high stakes testing has turned modern educators into job security and funding professionals. The risk of veering off the structured curriculum timeline to experiment with a new tool or pedagogy is often a risk teachers cannot take.

Today's teachers are facing pay cuts or more severe, job loss if standardized test scores do not meet administrative expectations. If you want technology integration to be effective, then give them assurances that test scores will be put on the back burner for a year while teachers focus on incorporating required technology. The staff members are qualified professionals and must be trusted and supported in order to give their best.

According to Work (2014), becoming a successful technology integrated school can be intimidating to teachers and therefore suggest the following five tips for those that struggle

### 1. Build a Tech Team

For those not familiar with technology, its integration can be very stressful. Providing a visible, proactive support team is critical for any technology roll out. Having a team built of teachers, support staff, and educators allows the campus staff to work with and support each other across grade level and content areas as well as serve as training resources to motivate teachers in slowly implementing technology.

## 2. Scaffold Effective Professional Development (PD)

Balancing the amount of PD with the needs for technology integration is one area most education systems fall short. It is often the case where overwhelmed teachers are feeling like they are drowning with all the technology changes and training while others may feel not enough is provided and become frustrated and isolated.

Having the technology team design a training schedule with staff input that allows for flexibility and "teachable moments" shows the teachers that they are being supported and valued while facing the technology hurdle.

## 3. Make Time

Finding time in an already packed schedule is difficult. Administrators need to carve out technology PD time even in the busiest of schedules. Teachers must be able to collaborate with each other for any successful implementation and student learning support systems pertaining to technology.

Professional Learning Communities (PLCs) are another efficient use of time while allowing teachers to meet, provide support, and monitor technology integration throughout the school year. This provides yet another avenue to support teachers that need additional assistance.

## 4. Make It Relevant!

Many older educators get overwhelmed and frustrated feeling that technology is being forced upon them and just use the basic technology required in order to meet or comply with expectations. Using technology to teach and successful integration of technology into lesson plans are two totally different things. A yearly PD plan that is relevant and meaningful is the best way to ensure implementation.

In terms of PD, approaches need to be differentiated and relevant. Much like students, teachers know their weaknesses, especially in terms of technology. Opportunities also need to be incorporated that are pertinent to curriculum content that teacher's will be experiencing. Faculty members respond to professionalism regardless of their technological knowledge. Focus on pedagogical needs when presenting digital tools and keep the language simple not "geekified."

Technology integration must be a school-wide culture and create a climate that allows and openness to take risks. Educators know that not all lessons go as planned. This provides opportunities to reflect, learn from, adjust, and press on just as we would expect from students.

Educators in general, don't need to use technology just for the sake of using it. They need practical applications and are provided clear objectives in doing so. The world is full of compliance requirements, and technology need not be one of them. The focus needs to be communicated that technology is a tool to facilitate learning in the classroom.

## 5. Encourage Them

Teachers, just as students, will still struggle even with the best instructional tools and support in place. What is important is that they are supported. The technology team may stop by struggling teacher's classrooms every few days and discuss or model new technology ideas. Attending occasional PLCs will not only show your support but also allow an opportunity to encourage and celebrate their successes and willingness to try new things.

Initially, focus on easy to use hardware and software and applications that are very user friendly such as those with drag and drop features. This will help to increase their confidence.

As with any illness, the lack of an overall technology plan in a school district causes a multitude of symptoms. A technology plan is "a high-level strategy that details where your organization is now and where it wants to go in the future with respect to technology and infrastructure" (Stockert, 2017). In a technology plan, the end result desired should be the main focus including hardware and software and which are the most relevant for the district/campus needs.

*Chapter 5*

# Attitudes and Beliefs

*The use of technology in the curriculum is a decision that ultimately lies with the teacher, based on their needs and beliefs.*

—Ertmer, 2005

There is often a misconception that the work of teachers is falling behind when it comes to technology, when actually it is how the work is done that has dramatically changed in the past decade. Electronic grading and attendance as well as reporting databases provide effective ways to disseminate information that is used to inform school policy and teaching practices. Digital devices and networks make it possible to share online resources within and beyond individual schools. This has expanded our interaction both for and between students and teachers as well as enhanced feedback opportunities to better develop assessments, lessons and assignment completion.

Although these measures were designed to ease the administrative tasks of teachers, it does little to assist the actual process of teaching and learning without proper training. Parents and society as a whole, relate technology and education as a way to revolutionize education as we know it. The reality is that we are still waiting for this to happen.

Much like trends of the past such as televisions and DVD players in the classroom, technology has been encouraged in schools and made widely available, but resulted in limited classroom use. TVs were often used during indoor recess or as a reward for good behavior and seldom used for learning or curriculum integration.

One such example would be the interactive whiteboard. While its capabilities range from making it easier for the teacher to structure lessons to allowing students with various disabilities to learn better, the majority of teachers are guilty of using it the same way as they did with the old blackboards or overhead projectors.

Past experiences in terms of pedagogy have found teachers integrating technology into existing practices instead of changing their practices altogether. The bottom line here is that the classroom teacher makes the final decision as to whether technology gets used for instruction. Research has published evidence that states uncertainties about which digital technologies produce results in the classroom which leaves teachers even more uncertain about which devices to adopt into their practice (Lim et al., 2013).

Technology integration depends on several factors and will vary from classroom to classroom. According to Law et al. (2008), the three key factors that influence a teacher's decision about integration include:

1. Leadership: As used here, leadership refers to the school principal. Whether a teacher uses digital technologies and relates them to student-centered pedagogy relies on how the principal prioritizes them on their campus. If the principal fails to adequately address and support technology integration, this can communicate that change is not valued nor a priority to teachers. If there is not a connection between what is valued at the school level and with teachers, the disconnect can cause serious delays in technology integration. The more benefits of technology that are shared with teachers combined with continued support in learning and implementation, the more value teachers will see in its integration.
2. Shared Group Vision: Few realize that there is a difference when it comes to beliefs about technology and actually teaching with it. Integration relies on how relevant digital technology is to the teacher's specific area of teaching as well as their teaching goals. Teachers must acknowledge that their teaching can be done more efficiently and effectively through technology including access to a wider range of curriculum supporting digital resources.
3. Technical and Pedagogical Support: As with anything, one's level of confidence with technology determines the likelihood of it being integrated into our daily work. Confidence, however, cannot stand alone and must be combined with a belief that one can troubleshoot and problem solve issues that arise in the integration of digital technology. For teachers with little or no confidence, the first glitch encountered will often leave them feeling even more anxious and uncertain about their technology ability and result in abandonment of technology use altogether. This barrier of low confidence is tough to overcome as digital technology is perceived as not worth the risks or negative effects it may have on learning.

It is a pretty safe bet that the majority of U.S. teachers today have been exposed to technology in their classroom. What is not a common belief, however, is that just because classrooms have technology doesn't guarantee that it is being used nor used effectively (Kadel, 2005). There are still too many teachers out there that think technology is a passing phase or a bunch of hooey.

Students' perception of their teacher's technology knowledge plays a significant role in their students' lives. When they don't understand how important technology is in the students' future and outside of school. Many students claim that if teachers understood its importance than they would incorporate more technology into their daily classroom instruction (Spires et al., 2008).

In short, how big a barrier to technology integration is directly related to the attitude a teacher has about students using it. Researchers have found that there is a direct correlation between teachers' educational philosophy and pedagogy and their classroom technology tool integration (Grant et al., 2004).

According to Ertmer et al. (1999), "Teachers who view technology as 'a way to keep kids busy' and who do not see the relevance of technology to the designated curriculum are unlikely to incorporate it."

For teachers that hold the "keep busy" belief, it is often the case that computer time is only made available after all classroom work is completed, as a behavior reward, or to keep a low achieving or early finishers busy.

As discussed in a later chapter, these days of high stakes testing causes teachers to fall into a skill and content priority mindset, which reinforces the fact that digital tools are not viewed as a learning extension to content and skills.

In the case of the campus media center, the same philosophy applies. Attitude of the staff toward technology affects its integration. So supporting the librarian in being more comfortable with technology will help impact the entire campus.

Instructional decisions are not only based on a teacher's beliefs but also upon their interactions and interpretations of the world. Thorton (1989) suggested that "teachers should act as gatekeepers controlling both the content and the interactive system executing decisions subconsciously."

Technology is one part of a teacher's interactive system and therefore plays a role in associating teacher beliefs with teacher actions. Beliefs are a key influence in teachers' choices about technology integration for instructional purposes.

According to research by Ertmer (2005), teaching that incorporates a student-centered approach in the classroom, have a higher incident of classroom technology integration. Student-centered approaches allow more choices in products created, control of content and are based on constructivist principals. Technology helps teachers access and manipulate data, gather resources, and enhance instruction that compliments the student-centered approach to instruction. Through technology, real-world context can be fully utilized, allowing students to construct knowledge through global interaction.

Kim et al. (2013) conducted a four-year study to determine how pedagogical and epistemological beliefs relate to a teacher's integration of technology. As a part of this study, equipment, technical, and pedagogical support and technology devices were given to participants with the target being to improve technology integration practices. Emphasizing the connection between student-centered beliefs and technology integration, the results found that the more student centered a teacher's pedagogical beliefs, the more ubiquitous the use of technology in their classroom.

In addition, Judson (2006) conducted a case study that focused on developing a deeper understanding of the connections between beliefs and technology integration.

Let's face it, when it comes to teacher beliefs, they do not occur in a vacuum. Personal experiences, cultural experiences, cognitive insights and critical images and episodes are the factors that lead to one's beliefs (Pajares, 1992, p. 310). The value a teacher places on instructional use of technology is the largest influence on its impact of enhancing instructional goals in the classroom (Watson, 2006).

In a study conducted by Wozney et al. (2006), teacher technology practices were analyzed using the expectancy-value theory. It was concluded that "teachers who showed confidence in their ability to implement the identified technology, as well as valued the potential outcome for that technology, were identified as those more likely to be at the high end of the 'technology user' spectrum" (p. 195).

It is hard to change beliefs when so many teenagers are strongly bound to social media. This mindset results in yet another drawback. Accessing their pages on Facebook, Instagram, and Twitter becomes a programmed, repetitive response including during class time. The frequency with which this distraction occur leads to the impression that teachers have no power in their classroom when in reality it highlights the social media addiction in today's youth. As you know, no addiction is good and rarely do they end well.

## Chapter 6

# Solutions

*Classes that have online resources and personalized curriculum produce stronger student learning outcomes than do classes that solely provide face to face instruction.*

—Harasim et al. (1995)

Integrating digital technology into their practice requires teachers to experience an ever-evolving understanding of what technologies exist and how to use them. Koehler and Mishra (2009) stated that "teachers need to have a deep understanding of technology's influence on content areas and how pedagogical landscapes need to change in order to integrate digital tools successfully."

Today, districts invest heavily in technology but often neglect to leverage in research-based practices while integrating it. In an annual study by the Center for Evaluation and Education Policy (CEEP) at Indiana University revealed "66% of students' surveys were bored on a daily basis in school and 17% of students reported being bored in every class." The cause of boredom was primarily stated as a lack of student-teacher interaction. "Sit and get" is a term used when teacher's primary source of instruction is lecture. Students commented that collaboration and group projects were the best approach to keeping them engaged.

So how do we address negative attitudes and beliefs of technology for teachers in order to integrate technology and increase student engagement?

## TECHNOLOGY INTEGRATION

As Inan and Lowther (2010) found, "Teacher beliefs is the essential factor that determines effective implementation of technology in the classroom."

In a study done by Ertmer (2005) found that provision of support, positive expectations, financial and physical resources, site and district administrative support, tech support, and professional development where all primary factors in teacher's beliefs and dispositions toward technology integration.

## MAKE THE UNFAMILIAR COMFORTABLE

As humans, we stick with the familiar because that is what is safe. Replacing routines can and will create anxiety and for some result in resistance. To decrease anxiety and ultimately resistance it is best to implement change gradually, giving teachers time to become accustomed to new devices and ideas.

Sometimes time frames and integration schedules require us to move quickly in training. During this time ask teachers for patience. Within the next few weeks of living with the new information be sure to provide support including discussion as to what is working and some of the barriers they are encountering.

These conversations can be great avenues to build an environment of trust and providing support through collaboration. In the case of resistance, don't ignore it. Recognize that there are very real reasons and validate them.

## REDUCE THE FEAR OF FAILURE

Support in taking risks and experimentation is the key to successful change during technology integration within schools. Being allowed the freedom of exploration allows teachers the opportunity to figure out which digital technologies support the learning that meets their instructional goals.

Failure is not something we as humans embrace happily. It often brings about hesitation and in worse cases, stagnation in efforts to grow for educators. Looking bad, especially in front of coworkers and students is an experience all would favorably avoid. With failure is the realization that an educator's career or possible promotion could very well in jeopardy.

Leaders need to be sympathetic and leave leeway for mistakes to occur during the transition and integration of technology. Confusion and misunderstandings will occur, and you must voice that and also that these mistakes will be accepted and addressed in a professional manner. Create a community where all are learning together which will display to all a climate of safe learning.

The International Society for Technology in Education (ISTE) suggests a three-pronged methodology in the achievement of successful twenty-first-century professional learning experiences.

Included in this methodology are the utilization of an effective coaching model, opportunities for collaborative idea sharing, and a fully embedded use of technology. Making learning relevant is the key in building positive attitudes in adults. Allow teachers opportunity to match their needs and interests to the digital devices and resources being integrated.

Millennials are adults of the early twenty-first century and are entering the teaching profession. Their learning styles have been technology driven their whole lives with an emphasis on collaboration. This must be taken into account when developing positive beliefs and attitudes.

Many of the millennials can be utilized as coaches and mentors to help support resistors. Modeling technology devices and uses will bring their strengths to the forefront and opens doors to building learning communities. Having coaches that are supportive and showing examples of teachers implementing technology builds trust among the teachers while building active communication among them.

## RISK TAKING AND CHANGE

Imagine change from the perspective of the teacher and what is at stake for them. Teachers are left to feel less confident or embarrassed about the new way of doing things and the frequent errors they are bound to make. This can cause feelings of being out of control and a compromise of their personal competence.

As coworkers and students begin to feel more confident with digital technology, those teachers that have not mastered skills, or must take time often from instruction to fix problems while maintaining classroom structure may begin to feel ashamed and shut down to technology integration altogether.

A second issue is that of learning goal and technology alignment. If digital technology is proven to benefit a teacher's learning goals then the chances of implementation are much higher than if this alignment is left unknown. This nonalignment lends to teachers feeling the risk of implementing technology is unjustified when compared to the time spent learning, planning for, and using it instructionally in their classroom. The problem is that many may view this hesitation as excuses or justifications to not implementing the technology

Regardless of opinion; these are real concerns that must be considered and addressed.

For these reasons, it is important for school leadership to provide clear expectations of and hold high value on the use of technology in their schools. For teachers who are already under pressure of standardized testing expectations, many will avoid technology if it is not held to the forefront of campus and district goals vision and missions.

Change is riskier for some than it is for others, but in order to grow, change is necessary. The more open one is to change, the more likely they will be to experiment and integrate technology in the classroom (Baylor and Richie, 2002).

With support from administration, change can be accomplished as they encourage and foster experimentation within a culture of change and at the individual teacher's pace. In technology, this means experimenting with new tools and approaches within their teaching practices and not being afraid of punishments or negative impact on student learning.

To accomplish this, teachers must be included in the decision-making processes about technology-related change and the school's vision for integration. Explicit information and modeling must be incorporated as to what is expected to be used, and how technological and pedagogical support will be provided.

Support needs to come in the form of training and materials, but what is often forgotten is providing time to play with the new tools, as well as collaborate with coworkers about opportunities to include technology into daily lessons. This pays off in the long run by creating an environment that reduces concerns about failure, uncertainty or punishment if the technology experiment doesn't work. As teachers become more comfortable resistance decreases and a positive culture grows.

Unfortunately, with the demand for more online learning and teaching with technology, and the decrease in educational budgets, resistance will eventually be coming to a halt or teachers will be forced to leave the profession.

Some direct approaches according to Bonk (2010) include:

1. **Incremental Change:** Change is never easy, and moving into the era of online teaching and learning is no different. Remember to take small steps. One example includes only making minor adaptations, such as starting with giving educators the task of finding online resources about a subject they feel they struggle with. Throughout the training, allow teachers to select from a variety of low-risk strategies and explore them. Many trainings give a brief introduction of the tool and then move on. Giving teachers this exploration time helps reduce risk stress.

2. **Shared Success Stories and Best Practices:** This option includes modeling examples of strategies that have worked for other educators. Don't be afraid to incorporate ideas from newsletters, CDs, Web portals, e-mail, or other digital resources to provide a variety of venues for teachers.
3. **Training and Development:** Choose one technology tool at a time, provide a thorough and explicit training of tool and examples of how it can be applied, and then give the educators a fixed period of time to experiment with the tool in their instruction day (say two weeks). After this amount of time is over, bring the teachers back together to reflect on their explorations and share how they incorporated the tool. Administration may even offer incentives for completing the experimentation in the form of certificates, stipends or technology give aways.
4. **Just-in-Time Support:** It is important for support staff to be able to help when needed. What often gets missed here however is that many only dictate a single approach instead of providing what is needed. Listening to teachers' needs and responding with options allows the teacher to choose which solution best meets their skill and needs. Another way is to allow teachers to select which technology training topics they are most interested in. This reduces the reluctance to digital devices that are of interest and therefore not supported by the teacher.
5. **An Atmosphere of Sharing:** To foster an atmosphere of change during technology integration, channels of communication and sharing must be developed. Let one educator share a technology tool they have implemented and discuss with others how it could be used in their instruction. One format example is Lunch and Learn where teachers either bring their own lunch or purchase a boxed lunch and watch educators present technology tools and share how they implemented them into their instruction. If finding a central location to gather is difficult, these sessions can be done through videoconferencing or Webinar programs.
6. **Awards and Incentives:** Incentives don't always have to cost money. For instance, for the teacher who proves to be innovative, may be the first on a campus to receive hardware or software upgrades, or chosen to receive new devices. For ideas that involve more integration or technology devices, a grant writer or mentor may be incorporated to work with specific teachers in writing grants for technology or conference admission and travel money. It is human nature to be competitive so use it to your advantage. Campus leaders may incorporate awards for online course development and innovation. This also benefits the growth of online communities throughout the district, state, and world.
7. **Modeling:** Utilizing the supervisors and colleagues of the staff is highly valued among educators. To see integration on their campus with their student population provides evidence that the digital devices and

programs can be used successfully. This not only creates opportunities for discussions but opens up collaboration about device uses that focus on specific content or themes.
8. **Mentoring and Coaching:** As record numbers of teachers retire in the next few years and new teachers enter campuses that are transitioning to an online environment, a cognitive apprenticeship format needs to be provided. One example is pairing a technology-savvy staff member with a novice teacher or teachers in order to support innovation and integration of technology.
9. **External Supports:** With the expansiveness of the web, external supports have become more important. Being able to access online teaching exemplar examples, instructional certificate programs, and degree programs make expanding knowledge just a click away. Through online newsletters educators can build a community including promoting online discussions with collaborative technology.
10. **Frameworks and Models:** Models and overviews are the keys to decreasing reluctance and resistance toward online learning environments. These frameworks provide a platform for reflection on what is working in technology and where educators struggle. With the abundance of information available on the web, frameworks and models allow educators to organize their day to day intake of data. Once organized, professional educators will experience a reduction in their apprehensiveness toward online environments.

If you have ever been subjected to change in your organization, you must admit that it transpires very systematically. With support through staff development, mentorships, and support resources, online interactions and decision making will seem less stressful for all involved.

*Chapter 7*

# Lack of Computing Skills

*Successful students and employees need to develop a hybrid skillset that includes both hard, technical skills and soft skills, like the ability to think critically.*

—Frank Connolly, MindEdge

According to the U.S. Bureau of Labor Statistics, as cited by Miller (2014), by the year 2020 there will be 1.4 million new computer science jobs. However, between current professionals and university students, we will only have 400,000 computer scientists trained to fill those roles.

It is often the case that it takes as many as twenty-five years to create a computer scientist. Even with the publicized research finding that computer skills are becoming integral for jobs in all industries across the world, a skills gap remains a major challenge over the next few years.

Although today many teachers and students can download music on to their ipod, use instant messaging or post blogs and videos, many cannot create a spreadsheet, attach a document or manipulate a word document, all of which are twenty-first-century skills companies are asking for.

In addition, according to a 2017 Library Journal survey, "only one-third of students enter college with research skills. Schools need to expand access to computer science curriculum and increase the focus on it in order to make it a central component in students' education.

So if these skills are becoming increasingly important to thrive in a global economy then what is preventing schools from incorporating computer science courses into the curriculum?

Students that are not being provided the computer science fundamentals are at a tremendous disadvantage. A lack of bandwidth to drive the necessary digital learning remains an issue in today's schools.

In rural and disadvantaged neighborhoods, especially, students do not have access to resources that would assist them in the proper use of digital devices. When combined with schools that don't provide the right classes, instructors and physical resources, these skill sets are not developed and can undermine a student's chances for college and career success.

According to a recent Gallup report in 2015 as stated by Williams (2016), many students are not gaining foundational computer science skills in school. The report reveals that

- 40% of U.S. middle and high school students report using computers every day at school
- 58% of students in grades 7 through 12 say their school offers dedicated computer science classes
- 52% report that computer science is taught as part of other classes at their school
- 43% say their school sponsors a computer science group or club
- 25% report they don't have access to a computer science class or club at school

You may think this number is low, but when you analyze it, this results in college students being unable to establish a research topic, design objectives, evaluate the credibility or properly cite sources.

This is reinforced by The American Institute for Research (ARI) (2006), that states "twenty percent of U.S. college students completing 4-year degrees—and 30 percent of students earning 2-year degrees — have only basic quantitative literacy skills, meaning they are unable to estimate if their car has enough gasoline to get to the next gas station or calculate the total cost of ordering office supplies."

Digital literacy is defined by the New Media Consortium (2017) as "a familiarity with using basic digital tools such as office productivity software, image manipulation, cloud-based apps and content, and web content authoring tools."

If this wasn't concerning enough, high school teachers as well as college professors are stating that many of their students lack computer skills needed for the new standardized tests being administered in today's schools as well.

Reality in schools today is that many tests require students to navigate between screens, type essays, and use word processing skills such as adding bold or italic text, and cutting and pasting information. This puts an extra burden on educators who find themselves having to teach how to navigate a computer as well as academically preparing them for the test.

Not having computer readiness skills doesn't just affect test scores however. According to Meyer (2013), students that lack confidence with their keyboarding skills will shorten their responses to short answer and essay questions on these tests. This may reflect as a lack of critical thinking, motivation or effort and can then be reflected in reference recommendations and teacher feedback for a student.

According to the Organization for Economic Co-operation and Development (OECD), 2012, 32 percent of sixteen- to twenty-nine-year-olds in the United States have no work-related computer experience. "This means that even though millennials have grown up on the internet, some may not be developing the tech skills needed in today's workplaces."

But it is not just students that are lacking digital skills. Teachers need more than the word processing and spread sheet skills of the past. The twenty-first-century teacher also needs the digital knowledge of cloud storage, social media, web and image editing, presentation software, and general multimedia understanding.

According to Elliott (2016), today's workers lack five main computer skills that are required for career success.

Software such as Microsoft is vital for any office job in today's market. Mail merging, basic spreadsheet, and presentation skills need to be taught which means that teachers must also be trained. According to Capital One and Burning Glass Technologies (2015), 67 percent of "middle-skill" jobs, such as administrative assistant or store manager, require proficiency in Word or Excel.

In addition, A Change the Equation study (2015) found 60 percent of millennials couldn't sort or search for data in a spreadsheet.

As for older workers, many do not have the computer literacy of the millennials and yet, have the basic office skills that younger workers lack. There is also a large skills gap that tech employers struggle with. Higher level tech skills such as software engineering and web development have more vacancies then qualified applicants (Hughes, 2016).

Many often think that if you know how to turn on a computer or can send an email, they are computer literate. This is far from the truth. According to James (2012), there are ten skills one must know to be computer savvy.

**1: Search engines**
Basic search engine clicking will only get you so far. Learning advanced search skills and learning how to determine good, reliable resources versus bad resources will get you a lot further in your literacy skills.

## 2: Word processing
One of the oldest uses for computers is that of word processing. Although many applications have incorporated word processing functions such as spell check, table creation, and working with headers are important tools to add to your capabilities.

## 3: Spreadsheets
When spreadsheets came on board, they were the believed to be the answer to everything and people were willing to fork out tons of money in the early 1980s. If you can master the formulas, references, and macros and rearrange them into useful easy to interpret information, then you are a valuable asset to any corporation.

## 4: Browser basics
Have you ever watched someone operate a web browser that was convinced they knew what they were doing? A search engine is not the only way to get where you want to go. Opening links in new windows, using bookmarks, and editing URLs in order to perform navigation as well as clearing the browser provides an endless world of information instead of sticking to a very narrow choice of website designers.

## 5: Virus/malware scanning
Although many anti-malware and virus programs are often included on devices, it is still necessary to understand how to manually check for these applications or spot signs on a device in case of infection.

## 6: Common keyboard commands
Believe it or not, copy/paste options can occur without a mouse. Universal keyboard commands make it possible. So if you are unaware of your systems commands, this knowledge may make more effective use of your time and keep you from ripping out your hair.

## 7: Basic hardware terminology
Misusing basic hardware terminology can be the difference between calling a network engineer and an Information Technology (IT) expert. In addition, all the cables may look alike, but they serve different purposes as with a HDMI or VGA cable and to be computer literate, you need to know the differences.

## 8: Simple networking diagnosis
It is well known that networking problems are the most common issues with computers. Although in today's world, you do not need to be able to

program a Cisco router, it is suggested you be able to do all if not most of the following:

- Determine your IP address
- Verify physical connectivity to the network
- Check that you have a logical connection to the network
- Find out what path network traffic takes to get to its destination
- Translate from DNS names to IP addresses

**9: How to hook it up**
Computer companies have gotten wiser over the years and now have color coded most cables and created unique plugs and connections so that anyone can hook them up. Even with this system in place there are still a high number of people that still cannot hook up a computer. For those that still need help in turning the system on, or plugging it in, you may be wise to pick up a class or take a training to do so.

**10: Security/privacy 101**
Digital footprints are left everywhere and many times throughout a day. Protection in today's cyber world is a must in these times of keeping your personal data private. Hidden viruses and hackers can hide behind the most average looking link whether it is in an email, or your bank. Knowing how to keep yourself safe is necessary in today's computer-oriented world.

*Chapter 8*

# Solutions

*I think it's fair to say that personal computers have become the most empowering tool we've ever created. They're tools of communication, they're tools of creativity, and they can be shaped by their user.*

—Bill Gates

The educational landscape of today is rapidly changing in order to fill in the gaps left by traditional out of date approaches and tools. For example, Khan Academy and Codecademy utilize online learning platforms that allow various talents to be picked up quickly. In addition, partnership between employer and academic institutions in order to offer online courses such as Coursera and Udacity with certification options is another approach.

Some schools are taking a downhome approach to solving issues by enlisting parents as partners during technology integration and resulting in increasing academic outcomes. For example, School2home is an initiative funded by California Emerging Technology Fund and The Children's Partnership. These two organizations have partnered with low performing middle schools in order for technology integration to be supported.

In order for students to receive their assigned device, parents are required to attend training on not only the equipment basics but also advanced topics such as how to check students' progress online, communicate with teachers and discuss strategies on implementing online safety and digital citizenship. In order to increase availability and attendance, classes were offered on weekends and after school while childcare and snacks were also provided.

Businesses for the longest time have relied on colleges to qualify their graduates for the workforce. Today's employees however are attempting to evolve the ecosystem. For example, The Starbuck's College Achievement

Plan is a program that attracts, retains, and develops talent that will benefit today's employers, by building adult computer skills needed in the current workforce.

According to a recent Program for the International Assessment of Adult Competencies (PIAAC) survey that was conducted by the Organization for Economic Co-operation and Development (OECD)in 2018, it was found that "adults without computer experience are more often unemployed or out of the labor market." It is because of statistics like this that schools need to better equip students. Providing them with the necessary computer skills that will in turn prepare them to participate in the changing economies of the future.

For twenty years or so it was believed that computers and internet-based tools would change education across the world. Since governments have continued to invest huge amounts of funding in order to provide schools and students with digital devices, programs, and network connections, the majority of today's schools have at least a basic Information and Communications Technology (ICT) infrastructure.

The truth of the matter is however, that the majority of students learn basic computer skills outside of school involvement. In addition, there is no definite correlation between computer usage at school and student performance, however, introducing computers into schools does provide opportunities and challenges that help students grow.

The receptionists and executives of the twenty-first century can no longer put off computer literacy. These skills are the difference between staying employed, being laid off, or worse yet, being hired in the first place.

The excuse of "I am scared of computers or I prefer to do things "Old School"" are no longer acceptable in today's job market, especially for older workers that simply choose to not embrace technology. So how do these hesitant workers bravely conquer their fears of the technology era?

According to Hoffman (2018), "A common stumbling block comes down to a person's attitude toward acquiring workplace skills." Many older workers are guilty of having a common misconception that it is the employer's responsibility for training the employees. This feeling is based on the belief that if they didn't need the skills before in their position, then they don't need them now. The reality is, however, that training and updating of work skills is the employee's responsibility, especially if they want to keep their job or move up in their organization.

Then there lies the dilemma of which computer skills a twenty-first-century worker should have. According to Hoffman (2018), the three main categories of focus are:

- Basic computer skills, such as using a mouse, typing on a keyboard, and navigating file systems and menus.

- Microsoft Office programs, with particular attention to Word, Excel and PowerPoint—roughly in that order.
- Essential Internet skills, such as email, Web browsing and searching.

The second part of this dilemma is how and where to get started. The first word of advice is to tap into the technology natives around you. Sons, daughters, grandchildren, or any person who has grown up with technology has computer skills, and most would gladly show you how to use them.

One suggestion for those who may be unsure of their computer skills is to visit a temporary employment agency that will allow you to take a test of your computer skills. The results will show you both the areas you are strong and those that need some work which provides you with a starting point.

There are also a vast range of resources for learning about computers and surprisingly enough, many are free. From highly knowledgeable people to learning centers, librarians, community colleges, continuing education courses, and online tutorials are available. The easiest place to start would be your local library. Many have computers available for patrons and even offer classes that are brief and free.

The main key here is once you begin to learn new skills, it is essential that you practice on a daily basis. As these skills become sharpened, remember to keep work samples to add to your portfolio and share with employers as you apply for jobs. This is especially important for older workers in presenting the fact that they are career-resilient and adaptable.

According to Derbenwick (2014), "While a comprehensive, long-term plan is needed to incorporate computer science education in all schools and to ensure that students are prepared for the jobs of tomorrow, there are five simple steps that teachers, schools, parents, and industry can take today to integrate computer science into classrooms":

1. Professional development

According to Roland (2018), no one knows better than the educator as to what works for learning. The challenges come when teachers look for resources that ensure everyone is working at the appropriate level of understanding, while also allowing them to construct learning in digestive chunks. These same principles should be followed when it comes to professional development.

The first step is to assess where the staff's skills are in terms of basic and technology integration skills. This can be done by distributing a survey or questionnaire. By using open ended questions in the inquiry, responses can be more detailed than if a drop- down menu or multiple-choice format is used.

Analyze and sort the data to determine which staff members need basic training and which need more specific tool integration.

Next, training should be designed around teacher needs and wants in order to fill technology gaps. Keep workshops specific so that teachers can attend only those that they need or are interested in.

Another reminder is to allow plenty of time for teachers to actually use the technology after it has been explained and modeled. Allow them to create lesson plans and activities based on their content area and can be used in their daily instruction. This constructivist approach to professional development allows teachers to not only see how technology can enhance their instruction but also assists in their retention of skills because it was utilized in a real-world relevant lesson.

Don't forget to offer continuous short trainings throughout the school year in order to provide information and support in small doses which helps minimize teacher's feelings of being overwhelmed. Providing teachers with helpful links to tools such as short videos or one pager help sheets allows them the opportunity to review or get help with something they may have forgotten.

2. Career education

Educating students, parents, and teachers about career opportunities for computer science degrees is also important. In addition to opportunities to work for large technology corporations such as Apple, these skills can also benefit areas such as healthcare research and government funding.

Computer science studies are perfect for individuals that enjoy deciphering codes, learning new languages and taking apart technological devices in order to see what makes them "tick." A curiosity of the world around them and the role technology plays seem to be a prime focus in these candidates as well.

Most computer science majors are very detail oriented and life-long learners which is needed in order to troubleshoot technological problems and keep up with the ever-changing role of technology. Of course being able to communicate and explain technology to non-technical people is definitely an ability that is noteworthy in individuals that choose this career path.

Some websites that can assist in providing more information about computer science careers and educational opportunities are:

- https://www.thebalancecareers.com/top-jobs-for-computer-science-majors-2059634
- https://www.learnhowtobecome.org/computer-careers/
- https://www.computerscienceonline.org/careers/computer-engineering/
- https://www.computersciencezone.org/50-highest-paying-jobs-computer-science/

3. Student incentives

It can be a challenge to motivate students to learn. In order to stimulate learning through online tools, incentives can be a huge help. Integrating free online learning tools is a great way to develop computer science skills and a terrific resource in which to tap in to is the Computer Science Teachers' Association at https://www.csteachers.org/page/Learning

After finding resources, the challenge of getting and keeping students motivated can be overwhelming. Plotnick (2015) has these suggestions for motivating students in computer science.

**1) Robot invasion**

A SPHERO SPRK Robot features easily programmable accelerometer and a gyroscope. Students can program the robot with drag and drop actions, controls and operations that allow them to give the robot orders. Connecting the robot's abilities to the content area being taught is key. For example, if you are teaching an anatomy and physiology class, you may wish to focus on robots that are used for surgery or training doctors and paramedics. If in a shop class, a discussion may include how lathes and milling machines rely on computer automation for greater speed and complex manufacturing. Information about SPERO can be accessed at: https://www.sphero.com/products

**2) Hour of code**

Providing many opportunities to expose students to the basic steps in writing a computer program is an ambitious but doable goal. One such resource in accomplishing this is https://code.org/. The idea here is to incorporate a one-hour block of time in which explicit training of software installation occurs. Coding not only teaches logical thinking skills but requires students to collaborate as they share and refine their code.

Other resources teachers can use to get started are:

- Computer Science Education Week (https://csedweek.org/)
- Code Studio (https://studio.code.org/courses)

These resources allow you to try the software ahead of time and have webinars that can be shared with students to introduce coding.

Parents can also play a role in the development of confidence in problem solving skills in their children by incorporating age appropriate coding apps at home such as Scratch and MakeGamesWith

### 3) Computers in content areas

Computers have the ability to be integrated into any content area classroom. Students can be shown programming and taught how to utilize this tool in their learning. One such example is in the case of a math content where a student is taught how to calculate formulas in order to solve problems. Then the student writes a program according to Ohm's law that calculates his physics homework for him. This not only demonstrates his understanding of the math calculations but also his coding and programming skills and their place in real-world problem solving.

### 4) Partner with an afterschool club

After school clubs very in quality and quantity across the nation. Starting a computer science club can introduce students to coding and other programming techniques. If this is not an option, then creating a partnership with an existing club can be another path that incorporates technology into the club's focus.

For example, to reinforce program participants' reading and comprehension skills there are a variety of programs that can be used that are technology-based and provide children and youth with practice in phonics, story comprehension, and vocabulary-building. Another example exists in a San Francisco school photography club. Not only do the students learn about photography, photo printing, and photographic artwork, but also digital photography software and darkroom picture development.

In addition, mentorships can be formed between schools and various industries in order to support the development of computer science skills outside the classroom.

### 5) Invite special guests

Invite local business representatives, family or military recruiters to speak to students. One example is to bring in a U.S. Army reservist in uniform and have them share that he is not only a part of the U.S. Army Cyber Command, but he also works at a local bank as a security consultant for their digital infrastructure. This provides students information that even if they do not attend college, there are other ways they can gain skills for technology careers. One suggested place to start in locating guest speakers is your local college outreach services. This opportunity can guide students in options including college course choices and internship and program placement options.

## 6) Field trips

According to Plotnick (2015), "Two-thirds of all programming jobs are not with software or hardware development firms. The vast majority exist with all types of businesses and government agencies." Why not combine this information with the fact that students love field trips? Real-world environments can reveal the dynamics of careers in computer science. Do not limit your options, however, to just businesses. Colleges also have computer data centers that can often be toured in order to show students the environment such as perforated flooring, battery backup units, and the miles of fiber optic and copper cables that technology requires. This opens up conversations about the types of work needed as well as the education required in order to create and maintain such an environment.

## Chapter 9

# Infrastructure

*A rising tide doesn't raise people who don't have a boat. We have to build the boat for them. We have to give them the basic infrastructure to rise with the tide.*

—Rahul Gandhi

One just needs to take a road trip in order to see that roads and bridges all across America are constantly being refurbished. In the same way, K-12 infrastructure also needs to be updated and refurbished. One to one learning needs an updated, robust Wi-Fi support but the downside is it comes with a hefty price tag. Another option is cellular support because of its 24/7 availability but unfortunately, the telecommunication companies don't always cooperate.

A third and often overlooked need is the human infrastructure. Today's world has become digitalized and any business whether education or a steel metal corporation will have technology weaved throughout the industry whether traditional to their roots or not. All future jobs will be technology based and it is time for education to catch up to the pace.

Furthermore, with the increase in the numbers of teachers and students accessing their learning needs online, the number of systems they rely on also increases. This makes it more difficult to track learning progress or know in a timely fashion just where students are struggling in order for the teacher to provide effective support.

So what needs to be done? Well, first and foremost a transformation in the entire traditional pedagogy needs to take place. To do this, teachers and educators must "buy in" to how specific technology will improve student success and prepare them for the digital business world they will be living.

Then there is the challenge of developing the skills and purchasing the proper resources to successfully implement a program that will achieve this goal. Just purchasing digital devices is not enough. Educators must have an understanding of how to effectively integrate the technology into their daily lessons and curriculum. This, however, is not an easy task especially for veteran teachers who may need to overhaul their complete pedagogy of how children are taught.

Another aspect is that educators need to be included in the decisions of what is required to ensure equitable access to technology not only at the school level but also the student level. "Classrooms need to reflect the world we want to prepare our students for" (Coghlan, 2004). Teaching and learning is going to be social, and the future is all about access. Our schools consist of not only traditional students but also those that live across the country and the world through online connections.

Professional development can become stale and ineffective unless it is continuously being refurbished. Random workshops and lectures that are not specific to educator's needs and fail to address real-world issues have become the norm in many districts across America. Professionals need training that will build their technology skills while also assisting the integration of the one to one in the twenty-first-century technology by tracking whether the integration is successful, or if improvements must be made.

Unfortunately, without adequate budgets or the necessary hardware, software, and internet access, it becomes very difficult if not impossible for teachers to truly integrate technology. According to Lantham (2018), "53% of public schools need to spend money on repairs, renovations and modernization to be in good overall condition."

"Although considerable variation exists, the average age of the main building of a public school today is about 44. That means many roofs, windows, boilers, and ventilation, plumbing and electrical systems need to be fixed, upgraded or replaced" (Berstein, 2016).

Many of today's schools, especially in low income areas, show the struggle of equitable distribution of education across the United States. As infrastructure continues to age and becomes more dilapidated, decisions must be made as to which areas take priority for refurbishing. Is it the lack of equipment and the unreliability of it that should come first, or improving the technical support or updating and remodeling the school itself? The truth of the matter is, doing nothing is not an option.

Another infrastructure barrier is insufficient access. Teachers and students need technology at their fingertips and are easily accessible. Therefore, it needs to be located where they are or having technology is meaningless. For instance, according to Zhao, Pugh, Sheldon, and Byers (2002) even though schools may have computer labs, the competition for lab time between teachers often prohibits many from being able to utilize technology. Even if the library has several computers, access can be limited by library scheduling and availability or before and after school which conflicts with bus schedules (Harwood and Asal, 2008).

The reality today is that learning does not stop at the end of the school day and therefore digital learning resources need to be available beyond the classroom as well. As stated in a previous chapter, low-income children in high poverty areas lack internet access beyond the campus walls and educators need to seek out ways to ensure that learners have access to connectivity and devices when they leave the building.

It is imperative that those making the decisions in education understand that technology infrastructure is the key to teaching and learning success. For those that are not technologists however, infrastructure can be a dizzying array of options including various network systems, multiuser software applications and cabling and traffic directing hardware.

District budgets cannot afford a network architect on their payroll which is why the majority of districts are equipped with incompatible and poor performing technology. Another issue is the belief that once the basic infrastructure is established, it will be there forever which results in support, refresh and usage fall off to the wayside and are not supported. This is why it is so important for all involved to have a shared understanding of the impact technology has and the expectations of its role in the system.

It is well known and documented that school systems are notorious for investing in one time projects. After receiving grant or bond money they often invest in a basic infrastructure and then neglect to fund the support, refresh and training needed for this infrastructure to be maximized.

In terms of the grant or bond money spending, when compared to technology infrastructure, buildings, buses and textbooks have a much longer lifespan in districts between replacements. So once the infrastructure is in place, the issue becomes that the technology upgrades are then left to compete in the budget with other program needs and replacement cycles.

The infrastructure needed today to prepare students to be successful for the future must be robust and flexible enough to support the continuously changing types of engagement and access of technology tools. According to The Office of Educational Technology (2019), in order to have effective and efficient infrastructure to support learning, a school district must have these essential components:

- **Ubiquitous connectivity:** Persistent access to high-speed Internet in and out of school
- **Powerful learning devices:** Access to mobile devices that connect learners and educators to the vast resources of the Internet and facilitate communication and collaboration

- **High-quality digital learning content:** Digital learning content and tools that can be used to design and deliver engaging and relevant learning experiences
- **Responsible Use Policies (RUPs):** Guidelines to safeguard students and ensure that the infrastructure is used to support learning

The truth is there is no glamour in funding infrastructure. It does not exist in a line by line item expense which leaves leaders making choices of programs due to cost or having the reputation of providing the "silver bullet" that will address their needs, but then results in not being compatible with their outdated infrastructure.

"When IT infrastructure issues negatively impact the ability to proceed on important curriculum and instructional alignment measures, the loss is significant. Marked improvement in achievement becomes less likely. Technology is then seen as having little or no instructional impact—and the ability to generate support for additional expenditures becomes even more difficult" (Gura and Percy, 2006).

One frustrating dilemma faced by district superintendents and school boards is the fact that the majority of these individuals do not have the level of expertise required to make informed technology decisions. This leaves them depending on technology staff or outside vendors for insight instead of experienced instructional educators. This creates a gap between what is truly needed and what is purchased.

The bottom line is that technology applications have become mission-critical resources utilized in running the infrastructure of school systems as well as supporting teaching and must be understood, planned, and kept current.

*Chapter 10*

# Solution

*The first rule of any technology used in a business is that automation applied to an efficient operation will magnify the efficiency. The second is that automation applied to an inefficient operation will magnify the inefficiency.*

—Bill Gates

A robust infrastructure for learning is based on a shared understanding of the goals and desired outcomes required to engage and empower learning experiences for students. Making sure all involved share a vision allows decisions to become much clearer about technology infrastructure.

In addition, schools need a connectivity that is reliable just as electricity and heat is foundational for an effective learning environment. Without reliable connectivity, opportunities that can engage students and teachers globally, or being able to access high-quality resources are not consistent.

So where do educational entities start their push for innovation? Well, small investments based on roles of modern pedagogy can be made in the learning environment. Project-based learning environments are replacing the outdated rows of desks with students sitting silently and staring at a teacher in front of the room.

Teachers are moving into a facilitator of learning role where guidance in learning has replaced lecture formats, and small group investigating has replaced students struggling on their own. The result is the need for today's classrooms to be adaptable in order to accommodate the changing needs of students. But how can this be done without rebuilding the entire facility?

Supportive microenvironments that integrate instructional strategies is the key. The problem is getting educational administrators to understand that having the newest technology gadgets and gimmicks is not the answer. The focus must be on utilizing the classroom space and digital devices effectively.

According to Proethean (2016), the top 6 day-to-day challenges of Information and Communication Technology (ICT) education in today's schools are:

1. **Restrictions on what you can download or install**

   Let's face it, teachers come and go on campuses and in districts just as the educational software being used. Providing them all with administrative rights in order to install digital resources is a daunting task. Platforms such as ClassFlow, allows your users and information to be stored on the Cloud.

   Cloud-based software allows everything to be stored online simply. It allows teachers to access everything from lesson plans and delivery formats to student log in availability in order to take learning beyond the classroom. It also decreases the need to use storage devices such as CDs or USBs as well as increases security by housing everything in one place that requires authentication to access.

2. **Blocked websites & firewall issues**

   Student safety, as it should be, is paramount in the education world. Before even exploring many of the popular websites and apps, however, school districts block access to teachers and students that are actually very educationally sound. This overzealous approach to safety really does more harm than good when teachers are already frustrated with trying to prepare their students for the twenty-first century in technology.

   In the world of dilapidated buildings and overloaded budgets the main problem with technology in today's schools is the device per student ratio, network connection, firewall issues, and student vandalism of equipment.

   Social media is the key in connecting to the best available digital content. Unfortunately, more time is spent discussing the threat of using social networks instead of highlighting their value. In addition, teachers that are more digitally savvy should communicate to network managers the need to seek out monitoring software that allows valuable content to be accessed without sacrificing student safety.

   Wi-Fi connection security is critical in today's classrooms including the use of data storage, email access, and handheld device usage. Online security policies have never been as important as they are today and it is necessary that these be updated regularly as technology evolves. According to Giandomenica (2018), "13% of data breaches in 2017 happened at educational institutions, resulting in the compromise of around 32 million records."

Glotzbatch (2018) offers ten pieces of advice to schools in their consideration of developing their cybersecurity and online safety approaches.

1. **Take ownership at senior level**
   School board members and leadership teams need to be involved in policy making to ensure that they are implemented and enforced.
2. **Establish a strong online perimeter**
   Firewalls and internet gateways need to be established in order to keep schools safe from malicious attacks and unauthorized access to network accounts.
3. **Update content filters, constantly**
   The largest portion that makes up the network is also the weakest link. Students are capable of constantly creating new ways to circumnavigate filters which results in the need for constant updating.
4. **Establish solid access control policies**
   A systematic process needs to be put into place for users' privileges to their system. Having a process in place reduces the risk of deliberate and accidental attacks. It is also suggested that the level of access for users be kept as the lowest level needed to do their job. In addition, as employees leave the district, their access needs to be revoked immediately.
5. **Check third-party providers thoroughly**
   Third-party platform providers need to have thorough background checks by schools in order to verify that security and safety approaches mirror or exceed the expectations of the district.
6. **Ensure secure configuration and patch management**
   The hardware and software being used on a schools' network needs to be common knowledge to all involved in terms of configuration, documentation, and implementation. Devices need to be set up so only approved users are allowed to make changes and update software.
7. **Monitoring and incident management**
   Unusual activity can be stopped immediately if schools continually monitor and analyze their system. If an unfortunate breach should occur, it should be reported to police and any other relevant authorities.
8. **Invest in cybersecurity and online safety education**
   Online safety courses are required by the Department of Education to assist in safeguarding schools. Included in the course should be explicit information as to the risks involved and the security policies enforced by the school and/or district. Follow up sessions need to be

held in order to keep staff informed of updates and possible phishing and spoof email attacks.

9. **Don't forget physical security**
Cybersecurity defenses need to be maintained in accordance to their importance and sensitivity with a focus on securing hard drives, routers, servers and other devices that store data. Cyber thieves often target school networks during summer and holiday breaks which reinforces the need for data encryption.

10. **Consider personal devices**
With the increase of student mobile device usage in schools and the incidence of cyberbullying on the rise, clear policies need to be developed and enforced on how mobile technology is to be used on a campus. Digital citizenship courses need to be integrated into the first few weeks of required curriculum so students know the expectations of device use, as well as, how they should interact with each other on social media.

3. **Cannot update apps/software**
Outdated devices and software are the norm for too many schools and are not compatible with what most children are using at home. Today's school budgets do not accommodate for the urgent infrastructure updates needed. Some schools, however, have adopted an innovative approach to meeting this challenge. Free software combined with "Bring Your Own Device" initiatives allows teachers access to the latest software, apps and educational content without adding anything to the budget. Free educational software suggestions can be found at www.educational-freeware.com/freeware/.

4. **It takes too long to get things fixed**
The most commonly used devices in schools are printers, photocopiers, projectors, and desktop computers. Unfortunately, the older these devices, the likelihood that they will break down increases. Interactive whiteboards used every day seem to be in constant need of expensive lamp bulb replacement. Color ink cartridge replacements are also never ending, and this is only compounded by the amount of time it takes to put in a work order and get these things fixed or replaced. This is yet another reason to use the free educational, cloud-based platforms which do not rely on physical parts.

5. **Photocopying and paper restrictions**
In my career, I have worked on campuses that put restrictions on the number of photocopies and the amount of paper teachers can use. The use of online lessons reduces the amount of paper schools use. Most educational software allows documents to be pushed to devices that students can access eliminating the need for a hard copy of homework or

supporting resources. Weblinks, videos, and online assessments also can account for paper use to almost be eliminated completely.

## 6. IT kit takes a hammering

The constant daily use of computers results in them becoming dirty and damaged. Often keyboards have missing letters, laptop screens are cracked, and tablets get dropped and quit working. This increases an institution's financial burden in terms of a budget that is already overstretched. This is yet another argument for incorporating "Bring Your Own Device." Students are much more likely to treat their personal equipment with kid gloves. In addition, this also reinforces the need for best practice sessions with students in order to show correct device use and care.

*Chapter 11*

# High Stakes Assessment

*Accountability makes no sense when it undermines the larger goals of education.*

—Diane Ravitch

National high stakes testing in today's schools comes with serious consequences for students such as promotion, retention, and graduation. Every Student Succeeds Act (2015) has put immense pressure on students, teachers, and schools to exceed expectations. What few realize is that with this pressure comes yet another barrier to technology integration in the following ways:

- *Leaves little time*: Teachers have even less time to explore new instructional methods through technology due to the majority of class time being devoted to teaching skills that aid in assessment. This is known by some as "teaching to the test." In short, if it is not on the test, it is not taught. In addition, teachers must also devote time to the testing process itself including maneuvering through the testing software or website. Between the benchmark practice testing schedule and the actual testing days, it is no wonder it is almost impossible to incorporate technology in today's limited instructional time classrooms.
- *Facilitating assessment rather than learning*: If that wasn't difficult enough, the schools that do manage to implement technology do it from an assessment standpoint rather than an instructional one. "As a result, the focus of technology use in much of K-12 education has not been on the use of computers for teaching and learning, but rather on the financial benefits of computer-based testing and the warehousing of assessment results" Bichelmeyer and Molenda (2006).

- **Results in fewer resources for technology:** Since the passing of No Child Left Behind now entitled Every Student Succeed Act, schools are penalized for not making adequate yearly progress which limits their funding. This causes a wall of tension between making Adequate Yearly Progress (AYP) and providing a well-rounded curriculum while also reducing available funds that would support technology implementation. Once the funding has been cut, schools turn their focus on accountability. "The teacher's role and the scope and nature of the curriculum is thereby reduced, leading to a curriculum composed only of what the students will be tested on" (Cowan, 2008) and what will provide more funding for future years.
- *Learning test skills instead of twenty-first-century skills*: With the increasing pressure put on students to meet higher scores on standardized tests, teachers are left with no other option but to move through the curriculum material quickly utilizing unmotivating lecture instead of relying on technology (Butzin, 2002).

Unfortunately, testing is not addressing twenty-first-century skills and leaves the perception that teaching, problem solving, and critical thinking is a luxury that classrooms cannot afford, and therefore are being ignored because they are not incorporated in the curriculum nor measured on standardized tests.

This neglect puts students at a disadvantage in regards to their capacity as workers in today's changing economy. According to The American Educational Research Association (2000), "High-stakes tests should not be limited to that portion of the relevant curriculum that is easiest to measure. When testing is for school accountability or to influence the curriculum, the test should be aligned with the curriculum as set forth in standards documents representing intended goals of instruction."

The Wisconsin Center for Education Research found that "less than a dozen states could accurately claim that high stakes tests are aligned with standards" (National Education Association, 2001).

In other words, even if the standards in curriculum addressed technology skills, standardized testing is not measuring them, creating a climate where teachers have no incentive to teach with technology since it does not impact AYP.

This focus on test skills in place of twenty-first-century skills also affects media specialists and other noncontent areas in that technology integration gets left off the table across the board.

**Scarcity of time:** For those that value integrating technology into the curriculum, they face the reality that it is time consuming to align the standards and goals to the curriculum. Websites must be previewed in order to become familiar with hardware, software, and program options. This additional time required to effectively implement technology often comes at a personal price of "teacher burn out" and can result in them leaving the school or worse yet, the profession altogether (Hew and Brush, 2007).

According to Applied Educational Systems (2018), twenty-first-century skills entail twelve abilities that are needed for students to succeed in the lightning-pace of the Information Age.

They include:

1. Critical thinking
2. Creativity
3. Collaboration
4. Communication
5. Information literacy
6. Media literacy
7. Technology literacy
8. Flexibility
9. Leadership
10. Initiative
11. Productivity
12. Social skills

## SO JUST WHAT ARE TWENTY-FIRST-CENTURY SKILLS?

Applied Educational Systems (2018) goes further by stating that each twenty-first-century skill is broken into one of three categories in which each category targets a specific part of the digital curriculum experience:

1. **Learning skills (The 4 Cs)** mental processes required to adapt and work in a modern environment
2. **Literacy skills (IMT)** discerning facts, publishing outlets, and the technology behind them
3. **Life skills (FLIPS)** personal and professional qualities of. Student's everyday lives

Let's take a deeper dive into each category.

## CATEGORY 1. LEARNING SKILLS (THE FOUR CS)

The four Cs are pretty universal for any job market and vary depending on individual goals.

- **Critical thinking:** Finding solutions to problems
- **Creativity:** Thinking outside the box

- **Collaboration:** Working with others
- **Communication:** Talking to others

**Critical thinking** is one of the most important tools needed to weed out problems and replace them with productive endeavors independently.

**Creativity** gives students the freedom to explore concepts in a different light resulting in innovation which is the key to adaptability.

This leads to a transition from things that may have always been done the same way and provides different outcome and scenario possibilities.

**Collaboration:** There are few jobs that do not require people to communicate and work together to some capacity. This requires people to compromise, listen, and communicate in order to develop the best solution to solving a problem. Although one of the most difficult of the 4 C's, once it is mastered, amazing things can happen even in the most dire of cases.

**The last C is communication,** and is what brings the other three qualities together, while also being the key for any organization to maintain success. Being able to convey ideas among varied personality types is a desirable skill of students of the twenty-first century.

While many may think communication is a skill everyone is born with, effective communication is the difference between success of a project and the project falling apart resulting in millions of dollars lost. With that realization, an understanding of effective communication is a required skill that students need to be successful in their career path.

## CATEGORY 2. INFORMATION LITERACY SKILLS (IMT)

These are sometimes called IMT skills, and are made up of three main elements of digital comprehension

- **Information literacy:** Understanding facts, figures, statistics, and data
- **Media literacy:** Understanding the methods and outlets in which information is published
- **Technology literacy:** Understanding the machines that make the Information Age possible

**Information literacy** is a student's ability to understand facts and primary data points that they may encounter online in order to separate fact from fiction.

Finding if information is true can be a full-time job in this age of chronic misinformation, and students can easily fall prey to the myths, misconceptions, and the outright lies.

**Media literacy** has more to do with identifying the sources methods and outlets in order to determine which ones are credible. Much like information literacy, it assists students to find the needle of truth in the misinformation haystack.

Taking literacy a bit further is where technology literacy comes in. Mobile technology and cloud programming are everywhere, and people who understand the concepts are in high demand in this Information Age.

Technology literacy is the what and why of digital devices. This understanding is crucial unless one wants to stay oblivious in how technology works and is necessary for students to be able to adapt to the world more effectively.

## CATEGORY 3. LIFE SKILLS (FLIPS)

Also called FLIPS, these skills not only pertain to someone's personal life but overlaps into the professional settings.

- **Flexibility:** Deviating from plans as needed which requires an ability to adapt to changing curriculum
- **Leadership:** Motivating a team to set. Collaborate and accomplish a goal
- **Initiative:** Being a self-starter to begin projects, develop strategies, and plans on one's own
- **Productivity:** Maintaining "getting more done in less time" in an age of distractions
- **Social skills:** Being able to communicate and network with others for mutual benefit.

**Flexibility** is one of the hardest qualities for students to learn because of its difficulty to comprehend that:

1. Your way isn't always the best way
2. Knowing and admitting when you're wrong

Showing humility and accepting that we don't know everything is a struggle for most humans, but even more so for inexperienced youth. However, being flexible when exposed to change is critical to a student's career success.

**Leadership** is the ability or skill that is required whether you are a new hire or a seasoned veteran in a career. Even the most entry-level position needs leadership skills in order to understand managers and business leader's decisions.

With real-world experience, employees learn to apply their leadership skills as they move up within a company or apply for higher-level positions with other organizations as they grow professionally.

As they lead individual departments, they can learn the ins and outs of their specific careers. That gives ambitious students the expertise they need to grow professionally and lead whole corporations. Although leadership skills are important, it is not enough alone to get ahead.

**Initiative** does not come naturally to the majority of people making it one of the hardest skills to learn and practice. Working on projects individually and during times outside of regular working hours increases an individual's professional progress while building work ethic, but each person has a unique perspective as to the rewards sought.

Regardless, initiative is an attribute that earns rewards that can be multiplied when combined with other qualities mentioned here such as flexibility and leadership.

**Productivity** is the ability to complete work in an appropriate amount of time.

It is also known as "efficiency."

Regardless of what level an employee is, understanding productivity strategies helps them discover how to carry out ideas effectively while gaining an appreciation for how others work as well.

Without **social skills** it is unlikely one will become a successful employee. Most if not all business relies on the connections a person makes with others around them.

Making long-lasting relationships within and between industries is necessary to be successful in the majority of careers.

With social media and instant messaging on the rise, human interaction takes on a different form then in past generations.

The result is a wide variety of social skills in our students, with some being far more advanced than others. And even fewer come to the classroom with the etiquette, manners, and politeness teachers are expecting in an educational setting.

So now that we have reviewed the twenty-first-century skillset, why is it we use a standardized test based on four answer choices in our schools when it is clear that employers want critical thinkers that can collaborate and work in a timely unsupervised setting?

Let's look at another perspective. As stated by Buckman (2007) "Higher education faculty are as horrified as politicians by the lack of preparation of the students who enter today's universities and bemoan the fact that in introductory courses they are often teaching the skills—writing, critical thinking, basic mathematics—that they expected students to have acquired prior to coming to college."

The lack of preparation and quality of the today's public school education results in students and professors both feel mired in catch-up. This is not to say that the students are not intelligent and capable, but most lack the skills that will help them become successful at the post-high school level.

Ok, so if the colleges are claiming the students are not coming prepared for college-level classes, and businesses are claiming employees do not have the skills needed for the twenty-first century, then just what is it that is being taught in our schools?

With today's teaching pedagogy focusing on standardized testing problems have only escalated not only in the classroom, but in the learning environment as a whole. According to Buckman (2007), "One major problem is that standardization has the negative consequence of shaping students into passive learners. Students do not feel absorbed in a learning process. Rather, they are compelled to engage in rote memorization which gives them no sense of attachment to or reward for the material they are being taught."

If that wasn't enough, it has driven self-learners to look for stimulation in other places via technology or worse yet, illegal means, which leaves the classroom being perceived as a generic venue of torture where students are not responsible for their own education.

Consequently, students are directed to give the right answer from four answer choices rather than thinking for themselves and becoming out of the box creative problem solvers.

## Chapter 12

# Solution

*Sometimes, the most brilliant and intelligent minds do not shine in standardized tests because they do not have standardized minds.*

—Diane Ravitch

Students need to be able to think critically, communicate effectively, and collaborate with diverse peers in order to solve complex problems if they are to succeed in today's world of globalized economy. In order to do this effectively, information technologies play a huge role.

Let's face it, in order to fully enhance an individual's way of thinking and working in today's world, twenty-first-century skills are invaluable. In my seasoned years, I have never come across a problem in my lifetime that has also provided me four answer choices. I have had to critically think, solve the problem, often communicate, collaborate, and think reasonably. With today's digital resources the processing time to accomplish these tasks has been reduced, but the skills needed are still required.

Schools need to proactively incorporate twenty-first-century skills into their curriculum. Based on Partnership for twenty-first-century development, Murphy (2018) suggested three ways for educators to incorporate twenty-first-century skills into their curriculum.

1. Twenty-First-Century Skills as Overarching Unit Standards

Within the curriculum map, incorporate a menu of twenty-first-century standards with the ability to check off the targeted skills and competencies within a unit. The benefit to this is being able to track which and how the skills are being addressed across a campus or district.

2. Text box for Reflection on Twenty-First-Century Skills

Incorporating a text box into the curriculum provides a space for teachers to reflect on ways the twenty-first-century skills will be integrated and the success or failure of the attempt. This benefits a campus or district in tracking which skills are being incorporated and help find those teachers that are successful and could possibly be utilized as mentors or coaches for others.

3. Twenty-First-Century Skills as an Addition to Existing Categories

Existing textboxes can be hardcoded to include twenty-first-century skills for consideration.

This allows teachers to reflect in several mapping categories as to how twenty-first-century skills will be addressed within the unit. This approach is a bit more difficult due to the skills being multidimensional and cross-curricular and therefore would require more adaptability.

Growing up and interacting with today's digital resources provides an endless amount of information at your fingertips. Generation Z and Alpha generation kids have actually never have been more than a click away from digital resources to gain information whether in their home, school, or with personal devices. These students are known as digital natives as comfortable with technology as older generations are with utilizing books and turning pages.

Standardized test results do not help today's students who encounter people online from all over the world and have made networking connections from the other side of the planet in a matter of minutes. If we do not transform this availability into a skill that students can comfortably manipulate in our internationally globalized society and assist in providing skills for success in their career then what kind of educators are we?

## A TWENTY-FIRST-CENTURY EDUCATION

A standardized test is not a twenty-first-century education. We owe our students an education that provides them the skills they need to succeed in this new world and the confidence to practice those skills. The outdated standardized conditions used today may have worked well in twentieth century as a way to sort and classify students, but to meet the twenty-first-century needs, assessments must allow for the flexibility inherent in the messiness of creativity, critical thinking, and problem-solving. There are three ideas of how assessments need to change in today's education system.

According to Reeves (2008), the twenty-first-century assessment framework needs to include the following conditions:

We need to use variable conditions rather than standardized ones. In a time when standardized test conditions take precedence over everything including kids' needs, and students are rewarded for their ability to perform rote memorization instead of for their creativity and critical thinking, we must give up on the obsession to compare students' scores on a specific set of questions. In its place, standardized testing conditions need to be modified in order to include real-world, relevant situations that people use to solve problems.

We need assessment that does not treat students like a herd of cattle. Where they are driven into the same kind of environment (a sterile classroom or office with either nothing on the walls or everything covered), given the same number two pencil, allotted scratch paper, a bubble sheet, and a set amount of time all in order to compare students by their score.

Few, if any, problems in the world occur in a controlled environment like standardized testing rooms. Students need exposure to solving relevant problems using critical thinking skills combined with collaboration, informational resources and digital resources that will prepare them for the types of problems they will face in the real world. After all, isn't this how we solve our everyday problems? We gather information, look at possible solutions and follow through with the one that best fits our needs.

We need assessment of students as teams rather than as individuals. Twenty-first-century skills are for the most part characterized by collaboration, so why do we test in isolated silos instead of with real-world problems? In place of bubble sheets, why not ask students to use creativity and critical thinking in order to solve problems in a manner that real-world people do collaboratively in teams? Working in teams allows students to analyze and develop solutions to multilayered problems and are not confined to one of four answer choices.

We need assessments whose content is public rather than secret. Many states, including mine (Texas) are super secretive and protective about state test content. Previous tests usually several years old are released to the public and contain outdated multiple-choice questions. This leaves students and teachers in the dark about what will be on the test and creates an environment where speculation rules. Every so many years, the test rigor is recalculated and the guessing game starts all over again. Teachers are told that the test is based on the state curriculum standards but it is so broad that is impossible to determine which parts of the Texas Essential Knowledge and Skills (TEKS) will be included on the test.

All of these solutions have one thing in common; they would require state officials making the decisions to give up their obsession with comparing student scores in a standardized silo.

## DIGITAL TECHNOLOGY IN THE TWENTY-FIRST CENTURY

Just adding technology to existing instructional methods is not enough. It must be used in a way that benefits students. With the rise in the numbers of digital natives in our schools, prescribing the use of certain programs is too limiting and does not push their knowledge limits. Educators must be open about all aspects of technology including hardware, software, and digital resources.

We need to transform public education from struggling to give kids all the information they need to succeed to teaching them how to take their own steps and go beyond their parents and teachers with confidence. A poster I always displayed in my classroom states:

> Education is what survives when what has been learned has been forgotten.
>
> —BF Skinner

According to Oxford University Press (2013), the four Cs must be a part of every lesson, every day in the same way as reading and math. Twenty-first-century teachers need to serve as a guide or mentor for their students, not as the all-knowing sage providing them with all their information. With so much access to resources of all kinds, children are invariably going to know more than teachers on different topics, resulting in being steps ahead in technology use.

In other words, the four Cs must be a part of every lesson, every day in the same way as reading and math. Teachers need to get over their self-perception that they are the all-knowing sage and serve as a guide or mentor to their students. The reality is that there is just access to too many resources in the twenty-first century, and often times the children know more than the teachers on different topics.

Today's teachers must be forward thinkers and lifelong learners in order to develop new ways of teaching and learning for their students. Approaching instruction from the perception of what students will need twenty or thirty years from now will move closer to the changes in education that are needed.

As Douglas Reeves (2010) argues, "Our insistence on comparing students test scores and standardization are serious obstacles to developing 21st century skills assessments. The old standardization model demands too many conditions that are antithetical to 21st century learning." The four Cs are critical in today's world, and yet the education system bases student success on a test given once a year on one given day in a student's life. Should a child's future endeavors be directed on one day's results or on the ability to comprehend, critically think, communicate, and collaborate in a society that relies on these skills to be a successful participant in this world?

As a seasoned adult, I am grateful that one day's unsuccessful attempt at surviving life's rollercoaster and meeting societal norms did not prevent me from pursuing my career goals and becoming a lifelong learner. Don't we owe that to our children?

According to The Oxford University Press (2013), there are five essential strategies recommended in order to develop a classroom encouraging twenty-first-century thinking and learning. The key here is to not jump in with all five at once, but to take small, steady steps toward the ultimate goal of a twenty-first-century classroom environment.

1. "Let your students lead the learning"

    Creating an environment in which students feel empowered and teachers serve as moderators or facilitators of learning helps to develop lifelong learners.

2. "Create an inquiry-based classroom environment"

    When students feel safe to take risks, they are more apt to ask questions and think out loud to find answers. This creates a self-motivated inquiry-based environment leaving students to lead their own learning.

3. "Encourage collaboration"

    Humans, by nature, are social beings, and a healthy active classroom is where collaboration thrives. Providing opportunities for students to work in pairs or small groups encourages the development of speaking and listening skills as well as collaborative team work to come up with solutions and achieve goals.

4. "Develop critical thinking skills"

    Critical thinking skills are more than simply comprehending information. It is where students combine these strategies with making judgments, analyzing evidence and combining information in order to solve real-world problems. It is important to incorporate activities into your lessons that will build students' critical thinking skills on a daily basis.

5. "Encourage creativity"

    It is important that the teacher be comfortable with encouraging creativity and incorporating creative activities into their lessons. Remind yourself that these types of lessons will remain with students long after they have forgotten memorized facts.

These five strategies need to be included in each and every lesson in order to develop twenty-first-century skills in our students. This may be new to not only the teachers but also the students and therefore all involved may need to adjust to this new way of learning. Once exposed to and practiced by students, they will begin asking questions, seeking answers, and become much more creative as they express themselves.

As Reeves (2010) points out, "Educational leaders cannot talk about the need for collaboration, problem-solving, critical thinking, and creativity and at the same time leave teachers and school administrators fenced in by obsolete assessment mechanisms, policies, and assumptions." Replace grades and test scores with personalized learning in which a discovery, engagement, and ownership mindset of learning provides students with the motivation to grow. In other words, focus on a student's mastery of learning not on a number of correct answers.

A successful school today needs to assess students in a variety of ways. Portfolios are one such way in which a child displays their work and discusses with a parent and teacher what they have learned and how they learned it. This provides the teacher a better indicator of the level of understanding the student truly has.

One such example of this approach would be where a student attempts to solve a math equation, but unfortunately makes one careless error causing them to come up with the wrong answer, but can effortlessly explain the steps in calculating the solution demonstrating that they have a total grasp of the concept. How many times have you forgotten to carry the one or added incorrectly? Does that mean you don't know how to add? Standardized tests do not take this cognitive ability into consideration.

## THE RESULT

The truth is that skills like communication, critical thinking, collaboration, and creativity go beyond the workplace and have been the anchor in the most difficult times in people's lives. Imagine a world where students have been taught the ability to think critically and creatively, to collaborate with others, and to communicate clearly in order to find their passion while preparing them for success in their careers, and also empowering them to lead happier, healthier lives. That is what educators should be striving for, parents should be demanding, and students should be experiencing.

# Conclusion

## *So Where Do We Start?*

Technology is not a faze; closing your eyes and ignoring it will not make it go away. It is a delivery method for learning and expedites educational content to students. The activities, assessments, and curriculum are enhanced through technology while increasing student engagement and motivation to learn.

The International Society for Technology in Education (ISTE) is a nonprofit educational association that has outlined the standards that are critical to technology integration success. These standards are discussed briefly by Soden (2019) below.

### SHARED VISION

A single shared vision must be agreed upon with all stakeholders in the educational community. This is not as easy as it sounds as everyone who is invested will bring a unique perspective to the table. All voices must be taken into account and heard of a collaborative initiative is to be incorporated into the integration.

Unless each voice gets an opportunity to share, technology integration will not be successful. Let's face it, we all want to be valued for what we bring to the table and in order for collaboration to be productive, each person must be provided an opportunity to articulate their understanding of technology and what their perspective of a successful integration looks like.

Some questions you may wish to reflect upon include: Will training be necessary? What are options for assessment that will ensure success? How and who will troubleshoot issues as they arise? Without agreed-upon answers, a shared vision will not be present and will handicap technology integration.

## EMPOWERED LEADERS

With every group of leaders, there must be one whose job it is to keep the shared vision at the forefront. There are times that the person in charge of making decisions needs to be revisited and possibly adjusted. Doing this frequently and smoothly often comes with experience.

Furthermore, individual teachers need to be given the power to adjust the integration of technology in their classroom. In turn, teachers who are empowered are more apt to empower their students which results in breeding ownership.

- This leadership model is far from traditional but does have the ability to motivate stakeholders to incorporate a social management shift. The amount of technology used is directly related to the situation at hand, and it is important to make informed decisions cooperatively in order to keep the integration practical while also identifying individual's strengths.

## IMPLEMENTATION PLANNING

As integration plans need to include several key points such as:

- How technology will be used
- The method of implementation
- How it will address the mission and goals of the institution

Professional development must also be structured so that it is ongoing and incorporates an assessment of infrastructure and the technology's effectiveness.

## CONSISTENT AND ADEQUATE FUNDING

Although every school system's need will be different, proper funding must be supported for classroom technology. Both teachers and students are affected when any educational area becomes under-funded. This requires a structured plan that incorporates funds for staff training, capital outlay, software and hardware, and infrastructure.

## EQUITABLE ACCESS

Of course a reliable network and internet connection is the key to successful technology integration. But in addition, equal and fair opportunities must be provided in order to explore new resources. There must also be a shared understanding of the term equitable access, which encompasses bandwidth but also trained staff in trends with technology as well as, where to access technology resources.

## CURRICULUM FRAMEWORK

An aligned curriculum is the best way to meet all learning goals while integrating technology. The framework most used when constructing curriculum usually starts with the identification of the key student outcomes and work backward in the building of steps to get the students there. This is referred to as the Backward Design which was introduced by Grant Wiggins and Jay McTighe (2005).

At the end of the day, any technology-integrated unit relies on the student outcomes it achieves. It is extremely important that a district's technology plan and the curriculum developed be cohesive with the state's technology standards.

For a curriculum to be effective, its delivery must be consistent and include explicit outcomes and expectations. Skills must be incorporated that can easily be transferred into the real world by students while also being developmentally appropriate.

## STUDENT-CENTERED LEARNING

The key ingredients to student-centered learning are accurate assessment and active participation. In order to accomplish this, the students must be comfortable with self-exploration of technology attached to a relevant topic. In addition, the teacher must also be knowledgeable about matching which technology is best for each individual student. Ideally, integrating technology targets higher-level problem-solving skills that challenge students and allow them to take ownership of their learning.

Technology allows for personalized and self-paced instruction that motivates and empowers students to take ownership of their learning. Integrating technology with a student-centered approach creates a pedagogy that not only allows for differentiation but improves upon existing teaching methods. In other words, "when students have the opportunity to work toward the same goals using different technology (devices, software programs, apps, etc.), they drive their own learning in a way that works best for them" (Soden, 2019).

## ENGAGED COMMUNITIES

Once technology is integrated at the school level, it is often the case that connections are formed and strengthened at home. Teachers begin to ask themselves if the tools they are using in the classroom transfer easily to assist the student's studies at home. This bridge can be reinforced and enhanced by forming partnerships with local business owners, local government entities, post-secondary institutions and other organizations to create more opportunities for student success.

With the local community support, technology integration can be supplemented with initiatives that build the business-school partnership. This promotes the idea that a student's education is an investment that is valued in the real world while also expanding digital learning resources. With the increase in community engagement, parents and family members are more likely to support technology engagement in their home.

I think we can all agree that technology definitely has its advantages regardless of how or where it's used in the classroom. Creating a unified front in order to address the barriers discussed in this book will empower teachers to incorporate twenty-first-century skills into their daily lessons and students to take charge of their learning.

# References

Adams, J. M. (2017). Don't slam the desk on the way out. If fewer teachers quit, the shortage would end. *EdSource*. Retrieved from: https://edsource.org/2017/dont-slam-the-desk-on-the-way-out-if-fewer-teachers-quit-the-shortage-would-end/58594

American Educational Research Association (2000). Position Statement on High Stakes Testing in Pre-K-12 Education. Retrieved from: https://www.aera.net/About-AERA/AERA-Rules-Policies/Association-Policies/Position-Statement-on-High-Stakes-Testing

American Institute for Research (ARI). (2006). National Survey of America's college students. Retrieved from: https://www.air.org/sites/default/files/downloads/report/The20Literacy20of20Americas20College20Students_final20report_0.pdf (p. 19).

Amos, J. (2007). Voices on student engagement: Survey of high school students reveals boredom, lack of engagement. *Alliance for Excellent Education*. Retrieved from: https://all4ed.org/articles/voices-on-student-engagement-survey-of-high-school-students-reveals-boredom-lack-of-engagement/

Applied Educational Systems. Retrieved from: https://www.aeseducation.com/career-readiness/what-are-21st-century-skills

Baylor, A. L., & Ritchie, D. (2002). What factors facilitate teacher skill, teacher moral, and perceived student learning in technology-using classrooms? *Computers & Education*, 39, 395–414. doi:10.1016/S0360-1315(02)00075-1

Bentley, K. (2018). School buses become wi-fi hot spots. *Center for Digital Education*. Retrieved from: https://www.govtech.com/education/k-12/School-Buses-Become-WiFi-Hot-Spots.html

Bernstein, J. (2016). Fixing our school facilities: An essential combination of education and infrastructure policy. *The Washington Post*. Retrieved from: https://www.washingtonpost.com/posteverything/wp/2016/03/30/fixing-our-school-facilities-an-essential-combination-of-education-and-infrastructure-policy/?noredirect=on&utm_term=.627753804c82

# References

Bichelmeyer, B., & Molenda, M. (2006). Issues and trends in instructional technology: Gradual growth atop tectonic shifts. In M. Orey, V. J. McClendon, & R. M. Branch (Eds.), *Educational Media and Technology Yearbook*, vol. 31, (pp. 3–32). Westport, CT: Libraries Unlimited.

Bonk, C. (2010). Overcoming the technology resistance movement. *Publication Share*. Retrieved from: http://publicationshare.com/Overcoming-the-Technology-Resistance-Movement-Inside-the-School.html

Buckman, K. (2007).What counts as assessment in the 21st century? *NEA Higher Education Journal*. Retrieved from: http://www.nea.org/assets/img/PubThoughtAndAction/TAA_07_04.pdf

Butzin, S. (2002). Project CHILD (Changing how instruction for learning is delivered): The perfect fit for multimedia elementary schools. *Multimedia Schools*, 9(6), 14.

CapitalOne and Burning Glass Technologies. (2015). Crunched by the numbers, the digital gap in the workforce. *Burning Glass Technologies*. Retrieved from: www.burning-glass.com/wp-content/uploads/2

Carey, J. (2013). How to get hesitant teachers to use technology. *Powerful Learning Practice*. Retrieved from: https://plpnetwork.com/2013/03/27/hesitant-teachers-technology/

Cavanagh, S. (2014). School districts using hotspots to help students connect at home. *EDWEEK Market Brief*. Retrieved from: https://marketbrief.edweek.org/marketplace-k-12/school_districts_help_students_connect_outside_classroom_with_portable_wi-fi/

Center of Evaluation and Education Policy (CEEP). (2008). 2008 Public Opinion Survey on K-12 Education in Indiana. Retrieved from: https://files.eric.ed.gov/fulltext/ED504571.pdf

Chan, K., & Elliott, R. G. (2004). Relational analysis of personal epistemology and conceptions about teaching and learning. *Teaching and Teacher Education*, 20, 817–831.

Change the Equation. (2015). Does not compute: The high cost of low technology skills in the U.S.—and what we can do about it. Retrieved from: https://files.eric.ed.gov/fulltext/ED564131.pdf

Coghlan, B. F. (2004). Addressing the barriers to technology interaction: A case study of a rural school. Unpublished Doctoral Dissertation, Department of Curriculum and Instruction, Mississippi State University, Mississippi.

Cowan, J. (2008). Strategies for planning technology-enhanced learning experiences. *Clearing House*, 82(2), 55–59.

Derbenwick, A. M. (2014). Computer science: The future of education. *Edutopia*. Retrieved from: https://www.edutopia.org/blog/computer-science-future-of-education-alison-derbenwick-miller

Dixon, J. (2017). First impressions: LJs first year experience survey. *Library Journal*. Retrieved from: https://www.libraryjournal.com/?detailStory=first-impressions-ljs-first-year-experience-survey

Elliott, M. (2016). Unqualified? 5 computer skills too many people lack. *Money and Career Cjeatsheet*. Retrieved from: https://www.cheatsheet.com/money-career/unqualified-computer-skills-people-lack.html/

Ertmer, P. A. (2005). Teacher pedagogical beliefs: The final frontier in our quest for technology integration? *Educational Technology Research and Development*, 53, 25–39.

Ertmer, P., Addison, P., Lane, M., Ross, E., & Woods, D. (1999). Examining teachers' beliefs about the role of technology in the elementary classroom. *Journal of Research on Computing in Education*, 32(1), 54–72. doi:10.1080/08886504.1999.10782269.

Ertmer, P. A., & Ottenbreit-Leftwich, A. T. (2010). Teacher technology change: How knowledge, confidence, beliefs, and culture intersect. *Journal of Research on Technology in Education*, 42(3), 255–284.

Fayer, S., Lacey, A., & Watson, A. (2017). STEM Occupations: Past, present and future. *U.S. Bureau of Labor Statists*. Retrieved from: https://www.bls.gov/spotlight/2017/science-technology-engineering-and-mathematics-stem-occupations-past-present-and-future/pdf/science-technology-engineering-and-mathematics-stem-occupations-past-present-and-future.pdf

Frank Pajares, M. (1992). Teachers' beliefs and educational research: Cleaning up a messy construct. *Review of Educational Research*, 62(3), 307–332.

Garland, S. (2014). How can schools close the technology gap and how much will it cost? *The Hechinger Report*. Retrieved from: https://hechingerreport.org/con-schools-close-technology-gap-much-will-cost/

Giandomenica, A. (2018). Top cybersecurity threats active in the education sector today-and why you should care. *CSO*. Retrieved from: https://www.csoonline.com/article/3250862/top-cybersecurity-exploits-active-in-the-education-sector-today-and-why-you-should-care.html

Glotzbatch, M. (2018). Cybersecurity, safeguarding and schools: What every school needs to know about threats online. *Beaming*. Retrieved from: https://www.beaming.co.uk/insights/cybersecurity-safeguarding-approach-schools/

Goodman, S. (2013). Learning from the test: Raising selective college enrollment by providing information. *Finance and Economics Discussion Series*. Retrieved from: https://www.federalreserve.gov/pubs/feds/2013/201369/

Grant, M., Ross, S, Wang, W., Potter, A., & Wilson, Y. (2004). *Riverdale Elementary "Learning Without Limits" 2003–2004 Evaluation Report*. Memphis. TN: Center for Research in Educational Policy.

Gura, M., & Percy, B. (2006). Technology infrastructure. *EdTech Magazine*. Retrieved from: https://edtechmagazine.com/k12/article/2006/10/technology-infrastructure

Harasim, L., Hiltz, S. R., Tales, L., & Turoff, M. (1995). *Learning Networks. A Field Guide to Teaching and Learning Online*. The MIT Press: Cambridge, MA.

Harwood, P., & Asal, V. (2008). *Educating the First Digital Generation*. Westport, CT: Praeger.

Hayden, K., Ouyang, Y., Scinski, L., Olszewski, B., & Bielefeldt, T. (2011). Increasing student interest and attitudes in STEM: Professional development and activities to engage and inspire learners. *Contemporary Issues in Technology and Teacher Education*, 11(1), 47–69. Retrieved from: http://www.citejournal.org/vol

ume-11/issue-1-11/science/increasing-student-interest-and-attitudes-in-stem-professional-development-and-activities-to-engage-and-inspire-learners

Herold, B. (2016). Teachers in high-poverty schools less confident in Ed-tech skills, survey finds. *EDWEEK Market Brief*. Retrieved from: https://marketbrief.edweek.org/marketplace-k-12/teachers-in-high-poverty-schools-less-confident-in-ed-tech-skills-survey-finds/

Herold, B. (2017). Poor students face digital divide in how teachers learn to use tech. *Education Week*. Retrieved from: https://www.edweek.org/ew/articles/2017/06/14/poor-students-face-digital-divide-in-teacher-technology-training.html

Hew, K., & Brush, T. (2007). Integrating technology into K-12 teaching and learning: Current knowledge gaps and recommendations for future research. *Educational Technology Research & Development*, 55(3), 223–252.

Himmelsbach, V. (2019). 6 Pros and cons of technology in the classroom in 2019. *Education Technology*. Retrieved from: https://tophat.com/blog/6-pros-cons-technology-classroom/

Hoffman, A. (2018). Get computer skills as an older worker. *Monster*. Retrieved from: https://www.monster.com/career-advice/article/computer-skills-for-older-workers

Hughes, S. (2016). What's hot (and not) in tech skills. *DICE*. Retrieved from: https://insights.dice.com/2016/02/01/whats-hot-and-not-in-tech-skills/

Inan, F., & Lowther, D. (2010). Factors affecting technology integration in K-12 classrooms: A path model. *Educational Technology Research and Development*, 58(2), 137–154.

ISTE. (2011). Technology, coaching, and community: Power partners for improved professional development in primary and secondary education. Retrieved from: https://www.ri-iste.org/Resources/Documents/Coaching_Whitepaper_digital.pdf

Jacobsen, M., Clifford, P., & Friesen, S. (2002). Preparing teachers for technology integration: Creating a culture of inquiry in the context of use. *Contemporary Issues in Technology and Teacher Education*, 2(3), 363–388.

James, J. (2012). 10 things you have to know to be computer literate. *TechRepublic*. Retrieved from: https://www.techrepublic.com/blog/10-things/10-things-you-have-to-know-to-be-computer-literate/

Judson, E. (2006). How teachers integrate technology and their beliefs about learning: Is there a connection? *Journal of Technology and Teacher Education*, 14(3), 581–597.

Kadel, R. (2005). How teacher attitudes affect technology integration. *Learning and Leading with Technology*, 32(5), 34–35.

Kim, C., Kim, M. K., Lee, C., Spector, J. M., & DeMeester, K. (2013). Teacher beliefs and technology integration. *Teaching and Teacher Education*, 29, 76–85.

Koehler, M. J., & Mishra, P. (2008). Introducing TPCK. In AACTE Committee on Innovation and Technology (Ed.), *The Handbook of Technological Pedagogical Content Knowledge (TPCK) for Educators* (pp. 3–29). Mahwah, NJ: Lawrence Erlbaum Associates.

Lajoie, S. P. (2000). *Computers as Cognitive Tools, Volume 2: No More Walls: Theory Change, Paradigm Shifts, and Their Influence on the Uses of Computers for Instructional Purposes*. Mahwah, NJ: Lawrence Erlbaum Associates.

Lantham, B. (2018). School infrastructure is in big trouble: Building new schools isn't the answer. *Education Week*. Retrieved from: https://www.edweek.org/ew/articles/2018/10/16/school-infrastructure-is-in-big-trouble-building.html

Law, N., Pelgrum, W. J., & Plomp, T. (2008). *Pedagogy and ICT Use in School around the World: Findings from the IEA SITES 2006 Study*. Hong Kong: Comparative Education Research Centre (CERC) and Springer.

Lim, C. P., Teo, Y. H., Wong, P., Khine, M. S., Chai, C. S., & Divaharan, S. (2003). Creating a conductive learning environment for effective integration of ICT: Classroom management issues. *Journal of Interactive Learning research*, 14(4), 405–423.

Lim, C. P., Zhao, Y., Tondeur, J., Chai, C. S., & Chin-Chung, T. (2013). Bridging the gap: Technology trends and use of technology in schools. *Journal of Educational Technology & Society*, 16(2), 59–68.

Lynch, M. (2018). K-12 schools need to stop wasting money on tech they don't need. *The Tech Advocate*. Retrieved from: https://www.thetechedvocate.org/author/the-edvocate/

Miller, A. (2014). Computer science: The future of education. *Edutopia*. Retrieved from: https://www.edutopia.org/blog/computer-science-future-of-education-alison-derbenwick-miller

Meyer, L. (2013). Digital divide: Access is not enough. *Transforming Education through Technology Journal*. Retrieved from: https://thejournal.com/articles/2013/07/10/digital-divide-access-is-not-enough.aspx

Murphy, A. (2018). 3 ways to integrate 21st century skills in curriculum planning. *Rubicon International*. Retrieved from: https://www.rubicon.com/21st-century-skills-curriculum/

Nagel, D. (2014). Spending on instructional tech to reach $19 billion within 5 years. *The Journal*. Retrieved from: https://thejournal.com/articles/2014/06/11/spending-on-nstructional-tech-to-reach-19-billion-within-5-years.aspx

Nekilan, G. (2018). Best apps for teachers in 2018 to download. *Education*. Retrieved from: Education.media

New Media Consortium Horizon Report. (2017). Key trends accelerating higher education technology adoption. Retrieved from: http://cdn.nmc.org/media/2017-nmc-horizon-report-he-EN.pdf (pp. 4–8).

O'Donnell, A. (2017). Overcoming the digital divide, step one: Increasing funding for the technology and internet access. *International Literacy Association*. Retrieved from: https://www.literacyworldwide.org/blog/literacy-daily/2017/08/21/overcoming-the-digital-divide-step-one-increasing-funding-for-technology-and-internet-access

Office of Education Technology. (2019). Enabling access and effective use. Retrieved from: https://tech.ed.gov/netp/infrastructure/

Organization for Economic Cooperation and Development (OECD). (2012). *Policies Towards Integrating Youth into the Labor Market*. OECD Publishing. Retrieved at: https://read.oecd-ilibrary.org/education/oecd-skills-outlook-2015_9789264234178-en#page123 (pp. 121–123).

Organization for Economic Co-operation and Development. (2018). Survey of adult skills (PIAAC). Retrieved from: https://read.oecd-ilibrary.org/education/the-survey-of-adult-skills/reporting-the-results-of-the-survey_9789264258075-6-en#page12 (pp. 72–76).

Oxford University Press. (2013). 5 Ways to prepare your students for the 21st century. Retrieved from: https://oupeltglobalblog.com/2013/10/09/5-ways-to-prepare-your-students-for-the-21st-century/

Plotnick, N. (2015). 7 ways to get students interested in computer science. *Education Week Teacher*. Retrieved from: https://www.edweek.org/tm/articles/2015/12/07/7-ways-to-get-students-interested-in.html

Proethean. (2016). Battling IT infrastructure issues in your school. *Resource Ed*. Retrieved from: https://resourced.prometheanworld.com/battling-infrastructure-issues-school/

Reeves, D. (2010). A framework for assessing 21$^{st}$ century skills. *Innovation Labs*. Retrieved from: http://www.innovationlabs.com/plsd/reading_materials/20100518121949459.pdf

Richardson, J. W., McLeod, S., Flora, K., & Sauers, N. J. (2013). Large-scale 1:1 computing initiatives: An open access database. *International Journal of Education and Development using Information and Communication Technology (IJEDICT)*, 9(1), 4–18.

Roland, J. (2018). Empowering teachers to implement technology driven educational programs. *International Society for Technology in Education (ISTE)*. Retrieved from: https://www.iste.org/explore/Innovator-solutions/Empowering-teachers-to-implement-technology-driven-educational-programs

Ron, C. (2018). Top problems with technology in education today. *TECHWALLS*. Retrieved from: https://www.techwalls.com/top-problems-technology-education-today/

Rosenberg McKay, D. (2018). Information technology jobs. *The Balance Careers*. Retrieved from: https://www.thebalancecareers.com/tech-careers-4161774

Schrume, L. (2018). *Learning Supercharged. Digital Age Strategies and Insights from the Edtech Frontier*. Portland, OR: International Society for Technology in Education (pp. 127–149).

Soden, B. (2019). What does successful technology integration look like in education? *ClassCraft*. Retrieved from: https://www.classcraft.com/blog/features/successful-technology-integration-in-education/

Spires, H. A., Lee, J. K., Turner, K. A., & Johnson, J. (2008). Having our say: Middle school perspectives on school, technology, and academic engagement. *Journal of Research on Technology in Education*, 40, 497–515.

Stockert, T. (2017). How to create a technology plan (yes, you need one). *Council on Accreditation Blog*. Retrieved from: https://www.coablog.org/home/2017/6/9/how-to-create-a-technology-plan

The New Media Consortium. (2017). NMC releases horizon project strategic brief on digital literacy. *NMC Horizon*. Retrieved from: https://www.nmc.org/news/nmc-releases-horizon-project-strategic-brief-on-digital-literacy

Thornton, S. J. (1989). Aspiration and practice: Teacher as curricular-instructional gatekeeper in social studies. Paper presented at the annual meeting of the American Educational Research Association, San Francisco, CA.

U.S. Department of Education. (2016). Trends in public and private school demographics and qualifications. *National Center for Educational Statistics*. Retrieved from: https://nces.ed.gov/pubs2016/2016189.pdf

Walker, T. (2016). Who is the average U.S. teacher? *NEA Today*. Retrieved from: neatoday.org/2018/06/08/who-is-the-average-u-s-teacher/

Wang, M. C., Haertel, G. D., & Walberg, H. J. (1993). Toward a knowledge base for school learning. *Review of Educational Research*, 63(3), 249–294.

Watson, G. (2006). Technology professional development: Long-term effects on teacher self-efficacy. *Journal of Technology and Teacher Education*, 14(1), 151–165.

Wiggins, G. J., & McTighe, J. (2005). *Understanding by Design*. Alexandria, VA: Association for Supervision and Curriculum Development.

Williams, T. (2016). Students lack access to computer science learning. *GoodCall*. Retrieved from: https://www.goodcall.com/news/students-lack-access-to-computer-science-learning-03794

Work, J. (2014). 5 tips to help teachers who struggle with technology. *Edutopia*. Retrieved from: https://www.edutopia.org/blog/help-teachers-struggling-with-technology-josh-work

Wozney, L., Venkatesh, V., & Abrami, P. C. (2006). Implementing computer technologies: Teachers' perceptions and practices. *Journal of Technology and Teacher Education*, 14(1), 173–207.

Zhao, E. (2017). Education technology: As some schools plunge in, poor schools are left behind. *HuffPost*. Retrieved from: https://www.huffingtonpost.com/2012/01/24/education-technology-as-s_n_1228072.html

Zhao, Y., Pugh, K., Sheldon, S., & Byers, J. L. (2002). Conditions for classroom technology innovations. *Teachers College Record*, 104(3), 482–515.

Ziekuhr, K., & Smith, A. (2012). Digital differences. *PEW Research Center Internet and Technology*. Retrieved from: www.pewinternet.org/2012/04/13/digital-differences/

# About the Author

**Dr. Michele M. Wages** is currently an Assistant Professor at Elizabeth City State University where she teaches graduate courses in elementary education and serves as the M.Ed. Program Coordinator. She has also served as an instructional coordinator for one of the largest school districts in Texas and an assistant professor teaching Emergent and Developing Literacy and Diagnosis and Remediation of Reading at Elementary Level to undergraduate elementary education majors. In her twenty-eight-year campus career, she has served as an instructional specialist on title one campuses, a reading specialist, and a language arts facilitator throughout the Dallas-Fort Worth area, including nine years on a bilingual campus with an 86 percent Hispanic student enrollment and a free and reduced lunch demographic of 96 percent. New teacher modeling and professional development trainings have also been a part of her career.

Dr. Wages received her bachelor's degree in social science and elementary education from the University of Michigan in Flint, her Master's in educational leadership from Texas Wesleyan University located in Fort Worth, Texas, and her doctorate degree in curriculum and instruction from Capella University in Minneapolis, Minnesota. Her dissertation topic dealt with the effects of two types of bilingual programs on Hispanic student achievement in reading for grades 3–6. She has also authored the following titles:

- *Engaging the Hispanic Learner; 10 Strategies in Using Culture to increase Student Achievement*
- *Creating Culturally Responsive Schools, One Classroom at a Time*
- *Culture, Poverty and Education; What's Happening in Today's Schools?*

- *Parent Involvement; Collaboration Is the Key for Every Child's Success*
- *No One Left Standing: Will the Rewrite of NCLB be Enough?*

Michele currently resides in Fort Worth, Texas, and travels to many states as a consultant and trainer of culturally responsive teaching strategies.

www.ingramcontent.com/pod-product-compliance
Lightning Source LLC
Chambersburg PA
CBHW032031230426
43671CB00005B/273